DIVING
CLUB MED

BY MICHEL VERDURE

AQUA QUEST PUBLICATIONS, INC. ▪ NEW YORK

PUBLISHER'S NOTE

The Aqua Quest *Diving* series offers extensive information on dive sites as well as topside activities.

At the time of publication, the information contained in this book was determined to be as accurate and up-to-date as possible. The reader should bear in mind, however, that dive site terrain and landmarks change due to weather or construction. In addition, new dive shops, restaurants, hotels and stores can open and existing ones close. Telephone numbers are subject to change as are government regulations.

While the publisher acknowledges the cooperation of Club Med, this book was produced independent of Club Med, both financially and editorially.

The publisher welcomes the reader's comments and assistance to help ensure the accuracy of future editions of this book.

Good diving and enjoy your stay!

Library of Congress Cataloging-in-Publication Data

Verdure, Michel, 1956-
  Diving Club Med / by Michel Verdure.
      p.   cm.   — (Aqua Quest diving series)
  Includes index.
  ISBN 1-881652-00-9 : $18.95
  1. Scuba diving—Caribbean Area—Guidebooks.
  2. Scuba diving—Mexico—Guidebooks. 3. Caribbean
  Area—Guidebooks. 4. Mexico—Guidebooks. 5. Club
  Méditerranée. I. Title. II. Series.
GV840.S78V47   1993
797.2'3—dc20
                                        93-16832
                                        CIP

Club Med and Club Méditerranée are trademarks registered at the U.S. Patents and Trademarks Office.

Club Med 1's country of registry is the Bahamas; *Club Med 2*'s country of registry is Wallis and Futuna.

Club Med Sales, Inc. does not own, manage, control or operate any transportation vehicle, any village, ship, hotel or restaurant, or any other supplier of services.

Club Méditerranée S.A., Club Med, Inc., Club Med Sales, Inc. and their affiliates reserve the right to withdraw, alter, or otherwise modify village availabilities, tours, itineraries, specific programs, sports facilities or activities at any time and without notice, except as provided by governmental regulations. All services are subject to the laws of the country in which they are provided.

Cover: Large Napoleon wrasses are found in the Pacific waters of Moorea and can easily be approached by divers.

Title page: The Club Med village of Moorea is nestled on a point overlooking a beautiful turquoise lagoon.

Photographs on pages 10, 11 and 15 are courtesy of Club Med. All other photographs are by the author.

Design by Richard Liu.
Maps by Justin Valdes.

Printed in Hong Kong
10 9 8 7 6 5 4 3 2 1

ACKNOWLEDGEMENTS

Special thanks for the enthusiastic support of this project to Jean Luc Oizan Chapon, Jean Michel Landau, Amal Benaissa, Jeff Bynens, Stevo Schwartz and Edwina Arnold from Club Med. I would also like to thank the many *G.O.'s* in the villages I visited for their kindness and cooperation. Thanks also go to Julius Pignataro and Chris Davies of Sea and Sea, Frank Fennell and Cathy Lawless of Nikon, and John Paul of Aquavision. Colin Tozer at the Riding Rock Inn and Domenick Propati at K+L in New York were also very helpful. Many thanks as well to Scubapro and Henderson.

DEDICATION

To my understanding wife, Bianca, and my daughter, Samantha, for their patience.

CONTENTS

FOREWORD

From its inception over 40 years ago, Club
Med has emphasized sports, especially water
sports. Today, with locations in the Caribbean,
Mexico and the South Pacific, the "American
sector" of Club Med offers a tremendous
variety of scuba diving and snorkeling.

This book includes a chapter on ten
locations with scuba diving, including the
cruise ship *Club Med 1*. Besides local history
and the unique ambiance of each village, I
have described a selection of dive sites typical
of each region.

For divers wanting to combine diving with
the varied activities of a tropical resort, the
experience of a Club Med vacation is hard to
beat.

Serious divers will welcome the recent
adoption of Club Med's Dedicated Diver
Program which offers up to three dives a day.
And all divers, as well as those who want to try
diving, will appreciate the newly upgraded
equipment and boats, and the availability of
PADI and NAUI certification.

The information in this book will enhance
your stay with Club Med, and prove invaluable
in selecting your next diving vacation.

Michel Verdure
July 1993

CHAPTER I HISTORY

THE PAST

The idea for Club Med began in post-war Europe when Gérard Blitz, a Belgian water polo champion, envisioned building vacation villages which would be affordable for all.

Shortly thereafter Blitz met Gilbert Trigano whose family business near Paris included supplying tents to vacationers. Trigano was enthused with Blitz's idea and helped his dream become a reality. The first Club Méditerranée village opened in 1950 on the Spanish island of Majorca. In the early villages vacationers slept in army surplus tents, and shared in the cooking, cleaning and general responsibilities of the campsite. From the beginning there was a strong emphasis on sporting activities. In 1954, with Gilbert Trigano joining the company full time, the tents and the camp atmosphere of the first villages were left behind with the first Polynesian-style village opening on the Greek island of Corfu.

By 1957 Club Med had become a limited company. Gilbert Trigano became managing director of the Club in 1963 (Gérard Blitz remained as honorary president) and continues to head the company, which went public in 1966. Although much of the day to day operations are now managed by his son Serge, Gilbert Trigano is still Club Med's guiding force and visionary.

The Club's first entry into the American market was the opening of a village in Guadeloupe in 1968, as well as the establishment of an executive office in New York. One year later, Club Med opened Buccaneer's Creek in Martinique and Bora Bora, a very small village in French Polynesia.

It took four years for the next village to open: La Caravelle in Guadeloupe. After that, expansion continued at a rapid rate: in 1974 Club Med built its first village in Mexico, Playa Blanca on the Pacific coast; Cancun was inaugurated two years later followed by Paradise Island in the Bahamas. And in December 1992, the impressive Columbus Isle village in the Bahamas opened its doors as the newest Dedicated Dive Center. By 1993, their 25th anniversary in North America, Club Med had 17 villages in the American sector as well as the luxurious *Club Med 1* sailing cruise ship.

Club Med began on the Mediterranean Sea in 1950 with little more than army surplus and enthusiasm.

Club Med vacations are known for their friendly fun.

THE CONCEPT

The original Club Med idea was to create an environment completely different from daily life, where guests could partake in a full range of recreational options without having to worry about extra charges. The concept included the all-inclusive vacation package where guests pay a single fee that covers transportation, lodging, three meals a day, wine and beer with lunch and dinner, most sports and leisure activities, and evening entertainment. In 1954, the Club invented its own currency—popit beads—that can be worn around the neck or as a bracelet, and used to pay for drinks at the bar.

From the start, guests had a special designation—*Gentils Membres* (nice members). The term *Gentils Organizateurs* (nice organizers) was used for employees. The terms *G.M.* and *G.O.* have become part of the international language of Club Med. The *Gentils Organizateurs* are the life and soul of every Club Med village. When not working as sports instructors, entertainers, chefs, hostesses or administrators, they participate in the daily life of the village, mixing with Club members. *G.O.'s* come from more than 50 countries and are moved to a new village every six months. In keeping with the all-inclusive nature of a Club Med vacation, *G.O.'s* never accept tips.

CLUB MED TODAY

There are now over 110 Clubs in 36 countries on six continents. From its beginnings of thatched huts and tents, Club Med has evolved to modern hotels and bungalows, but the spirit and philosophy remain the same: simplifying as much as possible the vacation experience. A respect for the natural environment dominates the development of the villages, and great care is taken to ensure that the village reflects each country's indigenous atmosphere.

Some changes are inevitable. For example, in some villages the Club has replaced the bar necklace with a memory card. With this card members can pay for their optional purchases within the village.

Since the mid-1980's, larger rooms, door keys and security boxes have been introduced in all American sector villages. At two of these villages there are in-room phones and TV's.

A far cry from its more primitive beginning, the new Club Med village of Columbus Isle in the Bahamas is decorated with art from around the world.

Where a week was once the minimum length of stay, *G.M.'s* can now stay for shorter periods if they choose.

The central dining rooms with their tables for eight have been supplemented with small specialty restaurants with tables for two or more. All villages in the American sector have at least two specialty restaurants serving menus differing from the main dining room.

Great food has always been an important feature of all Club Med vacations, and by popular request, there are now non-fat, lite and vegetarian choices available in the American sector when dining from the abundant buffets. A special coding system has been developed so vacationers can follow their dietary choices when dining from the Club's abundant buffets or in the specialty restaurants.

While some Club Med villages are oriented towards singles and couples, many locations provide special facilities for children. Within the village, there may be a Baby Club, a Mini

Club, and a Kid's Club for children 4 months through 11 years old. Here they will find their own facilities, from swimming pools to restaurants. They are cared for by specially trained *G.O.'s*.

Club Med is the world's largest sports center, catering equally to the serious athlete and the novice. Use of the Club's ample supply of first-rate sports equipment and facilities, as well as expert group instruction, are included as part of the vacation package. Depending on the village, *G.M.'s* can participate in a range of sports including swimming, sailing, wind surfing, water skiing, scuba diving, kayaking, tennis, soccer, body building, archery, aerobics, bicycling, and even circus skills such as trapeze, trampoline, high wire and juggling. An artificial climbing wall to teach rock climbing skills was recently added at Playa Blanca, Mexico. A small fee is charged for golf, deep-sea fishing and horseback riding, as well as for rental of ski equipment at the Club's mountain resorts.

Club Med brings people together from different social, national and cultural backgrounds, and provides an atmosphere of easy camaraderie removed from the responsibilities of everyday life. You can participate in as many activities as you want, or do nothing but relax in solitude.

Wind surfing is one of the many water sports offered at Club Med.

Dining at Club Med is luscious and abundant as guests feast on local and international delicacies.

CHAPTER **II** DIVING

A lot has changed in the Club Med diving program in the last several years. Gone are the days of J-valves with pull rods, no pressure or depth gauges, and antiquated equipment. Where once even certified instructors had to undergo a "check out dive" and be shepherded on dives by Club Med staff, now C-cards from U.S. agencies are accepted and certified divers can dive as a buddy team. Equipment is now top of the line—Scubapro, Beuchat and Henderson—with different colors for size. Tanks are color coded as well with blue for the first dive and pink for the second. Boats have also been upgraded, and the Club Med fleet now boasts some of the newest and most comfortable dive boats available. Besides the

Club Med resort course, many Club Med villages now offer PADI and NAUI open water and advanced courses, and up to three dives a day.

All these changes came about with the implementation of the Dedicated Diver Program at selected Dedicated Dive Centers, the first of which was Turkoise in 1988. This program was designed specifically to cater to more experienced divers who want to combine a great dive trip with the other amenities of a Club Med vacation.

There are currently 10 Club Med villages (including the *Club Med 1*) in the American sector that offer scuba programs. A chapter is devoted to each of these villages, which fall into one the four categories listed below.

DEDICATED DIVE CENTERS

Turkoise, St. Lucia, Columbus Isle, Sonora Bay and Moorea

The dive program consists of two morning open water dives with an optional afternoon dive (except at Moorea) for an additional fee. There is one night dive a week. The first dive of the week is usually shallow and accompanied by an instructor to let those divers who haven't recently been in the water get reacquainted with their equipment and new surroundings. After the first dive, certified divers may dive as buddy teams.

PADI and NAUI open water and advanced certifications are available for an extra charge. These C-cards are accepted worldwide. A variety of specialty courses may also be offered.

Gearing up couldn't be easier. Gear is color-coded according to size with different colored tanks for first and second dives.

A short stroll along the beach brings you to your afternoon dive lesson.

Dive boats often moor in lagoons where topside scenery is every bit as beautiful as it is underwater. These are the rugged peaks of Moorea, the volcanic island near Tahiti.

Nassau groupers such as this one at Columbus Isle are friendly and curious.

Snacking on fresh fruit after a dive is a welcome treat for all divers.

For those wanting less intensive training the Club Med resort course is offered for free. This certification only permits diving with an instructor within the Club Med system.

STANDARD PROGRAM

Martinique and Cancun

The standard program consists of one morning dive a day and one night dive per week for those with at least 10 previous dives.

The Club Med resort course is offered free of charge, but there is no PADI or NAUI training available.

TRAINING ONLY

Eleuthera and Playa Blanca

While there are no boats or non-training open water dives available at these villages, PADI and NAUI open water certification is offered for free, as is the Club Med resort course.

Dive trips with local dive operations outside the Club Med village may be available for certified divers.

CLUB MED 1

Certified divers only are permitted to dive from the *Club Med 1* and no instruction is available. Dives are limited to one a day. There is a brief introduction to scuba conducted once a week by an instructor for those who want to see what it's like to breathe underwater.

GENERAL REGULATIONS

Age. The scuba diving program is offered to those 12 years and older. Minors must have written authorization from one of their parents or a legal guardian.

Buddy system. A dive instructor is in the water with the dive group at all times and will lead the dive. However, certified divers are permitted to dive on their own as a buddy team if they wish. Minors must be accompanied by a parent or legal guardian unless they sign a waiver allowing the child to dive without parental supervision.

C-cards. Club Med accepts C-cards of all major U.S. certification agencies. Certified divers must present a valid C-card before being permitted to dive.

Depth. For divers age 12 to 14 years the depth limit is 60 feet (18 m). Other divers are limited to 100 feet (30 m) unless both divers of a buddy team have dive computers in which case they can go to 130 feet (39 m). All dives must be conducted within the no-decompression limits.

Environment. Buoyancy control is stressed in all training at Club Med in order to keep divers from banging into or dragging their equipment over the fragile coral reef. Interaction with marine life is limited to observation and photography, and divers are not permitted to touch marine life or remove anything from the environment. As an additional deterrent to touching coral and marine life, divers are not permitted to wear gloves.

In order to further protect the reefs, the dive sites are marked by permanent moorings so dive boats do not have to drop anchor. The exceptions are sites where the dive is conducted as a drift dive.

Medicals and waivers. Divers must sign a waiver exempting Club Med of all liability. Certified divers do not need to take a medical, but non-certified divers will be required to complete a medical history form. Certain medical conditions may prohibit participation in scuba diving.

Safety. Oxygen and medical kits are on board all Club Med dive boats, and instructors and divemasters are trained in emergency first aid. Doctors experienced in scuba medicine either accompany the dive boat, are in the village, or are on call. Evacuation procedures to the nearest recompression chamber or hospital have been planned in case of an emergency.

Decompression hang bars with an extra air supply are hung from the dive boats at 15 feet (5 m) and divers are required to make a safety stop prior to surfacing.

CHAPTER III TURKOISE

Turks & Caicos

THE PAST

Some historians believe it was a spit of land in the Turks and Caicos, a string of tiny islands in the Bahamas chain that provided Columbus with his first view of the New World. At the time, the only known inhabitants of the eight large islands and 30-odd cays, were the Arawak Indians whom Columbus called the Lucayans. They were a race of manioc farmers, fishermen and traders who had begun migrating northward from their original homes in northeastern South America shortly before the birth of Christ. It was in the Turks and Caicos, two distinct sets of low-lying islands, that the Lucayans found refuge from the Carib Indians.

As was the case with many other Indian cultures, it was the Lucayan's encounter with Spaniards that sealed their doom. Soon after 1512 conquistadors swept through the region, shanghaiing the fittest for slave labor in Hispaniola, where the Spanish were searching for gold. Untold numbers of Lucayans died of disease and maltreatment. By the middle of the 16th century, the islands' Indian population had been annihilated.

In 1540, when Spanish raiders landed on Grand Turk they found scenes of desolation and only one inhabitant: an old man. For years afterward, the island was listed on Spanish charts as El Viejo, or Old Man Island. The island's current name of Grand Turk, according to one account, came about because of a species of cactus whose distinctive red cap resembles a fez.

Later in the l6th century, European migration to the Turks and Caicos began with an influx of Protestants, mainly French, who had fled their homes to escape religious persecution. Some of the newcomers took up piracy beginning in the 1640's. The buccaneering era is thought to have begun when an immigrant

from Normandy named Pierre Le Grand captured a treasure-laden Spanish galleon in the region.

For the next 130 years, the islands served chiefly as hideouts for pirates and buccaneers such as Le Grand. During this time the major European powers were claiming and colonizing the larger islands throughout the Caribbean. In 1670 Spain ceded the islands to Great Britain in the Treaty of Madrid.

The agreement led to an influx of traders from the British island of Bermuda, who, beginning in 1678, brought in African slaves to start what was to become the major historic industry of the islands: the production of sea salt. It was produced from the vast tidal flats of Grand Turk and Salt Cay, and sold to British colonists in America. Thousands of trees were cut by the salt rakers and the islands of Grand Turk, Salt Cay and South Caicos are largely arid to this day.

Despite efforts to control the islands by the government in Bermuda, sporadic pirate raids and the wars of the European powers left little stability. Control of the Turks and Caicos went from British to Spanish to French hands until the British finally ousted the French midway through the 18th century.

In the late 1700's, following the American Revolution, Britain began rewarding loyalist planters with land grants in the Turks and Caicos. The new arrivals and their African slaves—the first permanent settlers since the Lucayans—established cotton and sisal plantations. But the islands' soil was too thin to

Certified divers can explore the waters of Turks and Caicos in buddy teams.

support cotton as a major export crop. By 1820 most of the settlers, tormented by biting insects and occasional hurricanes, had moved away.

By the mid-1800's, rule from Bermuda had become increasingly unpopular. In 1874, the Turks and Caicos were annexed by Jamaica, which had developed trading links with the islands as ships sailing between England and Jamaica often docked at Grand Turk.

THE PRESENT

The Turks and Caicos remained a Jamaican possession until 1962, when Jamaica gained its independence from Britain. At that point, the islands became a British Crown Colony associated with the Bahamas.

The Turks and Caicos are now designated a British Dependent Territory; Queen Elizabeth II is head of state, represented by a governor, who presides over an executive council. Two council members—the Attorney General and the Chief Secretary—are appointed by London.

Besides Grand Turk, South Caicos and Salt Cay, the other major islands making up the Turks and Caicos are Providenciales, North Caicos, Middle Caicos, East Caicos and West Caicos. Five of the largest islands of this group are separated from the others by the Turks Island Passage, a 22-mile (35 km), 7,000-foot (2,121 m) deep channel.

Although Grand Turk is the seat of government, Providenciales, or Provo as it is known, is the resort capital. It is the second most populated island after Grand Turk, and has something of a cosmopolitan flavor.

Modern development began in earnest in 1967, when the island's potential for tourism was recognized. There are now several medium-sized hotels on Provo, including Club Med's Turkoise which opened in 1984. In addition there are a number of rental villas, restaurants, shops, discos and full-service marinas. There are facilities for fishing, diving, sailing, wind surfing and tennis, among other activities.

Provo, 14 miles long and an average of three miles wide, is shielded from the Atlantic surf by a long barrier reef on its north coast. Beautiful beaches run the full length of this coast. A narrow ridge of limestone hills lies behind the northern beaches. These are called the Blue Hills from which derives the island's nickname "Blue Hill." The western part of the island consists of creeks, sounds, tidal flats and mangrove vegetation.

USEFUL INFORMATION

Climate. The Turks and Caicos, situated south of the Tropic of Cancer, have a subtropical climate. Average daytime temperatures range from 90 to 96°F (32-36°C) in summer, dropping to 75°F (24°C) in December before rising again to 75 to 85°F (24-29°C) in spring.

The trade winds off the Southeast Equatorial Current act as a moderating force and nighttime temperatures rarely fall below 70°F (21°C) during any season.

Cloudy days are rare, as is rainfall. The islands receive only about 40 inches (103 cm) a year, and water is carefully conserved.

Currency. The official currency is the U.S. dollar. There are no currency regulations, and no corporate or personal taxes. Travelers checks and major credit cards are widely accepted.

Electricity. Standard voltage is 120 volts, 60 cycles with U.S. sockets.

Entry and Exit Requirements. Visitors must have a valid passport with a return ticket and are permitted to stay for up to one month without a visa. No vaccinations are required. There is a departure tax of US$10 payable at the airport.

Etiquette. Casual dress is suggested. Islanders have a reputation for being kind and friendly, and religious. They frown on topless sunbathing and swimming, as well as blatantly inappropriate dress in public places—an attitude that conforms with Club Med policy.

Getting There. The main air connection to Providenciales is through Miami, 575 miles (927 km) to the northwest. Cayman Airways has flights three times a week, while American Airlines has once-a-week flights. Club Med operates once-a-week charters originating in New York and Miami.

Club Med provides transport to the village which is a 15-minute ride from the airport. Taxis are also available.

Language. The official language is English, although French is also spoken at the Club Med village. There is a growing Haitian community on the islands who speak Creole.

Appropriately named for the color of the water it borders, the sprawling resort of Turkoise was opened in 1984.

An interesting excursion is to Little Water Cay, commonly called Iguana Island, which is covered with friendly iguanas.

Sightseeing. There are Club Med tours to other islands in the Turks and Caicos, as well as cruises at sunset, under the stars and during the full moon.

Arrangements can be made for fishing expeditions, both deep-sea, and to the islands' renowned bone-fishing grounds. There are also opportunities for shopping forays and visits to Blue Hills, a typical local village. At the Island Sea Center one can view techniques of conch farming and find information on the local marine life.

Provo also boasts an 18-hole championship golf course, a casino and a variety of restaurants.

On the island of Middle Caicos, two islands east of Provo, one can take a guided tour of the vast network of limestone caves near the town of Conch Bar.

Just off Provo's northeast tip, a 10-minute boat ride from the Club Med village, is Iguana Island, a cay alive with friendly iguanas. Most are tame enough for easy close-up photography.

In the beginning of August, around the time

of the major national holiday, Emancipation Day, the islands sponsor a major billfish tournament, a regatta, a beauty pageant (to choose Miss Turks and Caicos), as well as festivities on Provo complete with a Carnival patterned after Mardi Gras.

DINING OUTSIDE CLUB MED

Banana Boat   6-5706

The Banana Boat, a restaurant overlooking a marina in the village of Turtle Cove, offers Caribbean specialties such as fish fritters and conch. It has a comfortable local ambiance, indoor and outdoor dining areas, and reasonable prices. It is approximately a 15-minute taxi ride (fare about US$15) from the Club Med village.

Portofino   6-5555

This is an elegant, air-conditioned Italian restaurant with a view of the ocean and excellent food. It is also on the expensive side. Located on the second floor of the Ramada Hotel—virtually next door to Club Med—it is reachable by a shuttle (US$5, refundable if you visit the casino).

Alfred's   6-4679

Situated on a hilltop along the road to Turtle Cove, Alfred's offers local food and pasta at moderate prices. Both indoor and outdoor dining is available—all with a beautiful view of the ocean. It is about a 10-minute cab ride from the Club Med village.

THE CLUB MED VILLAGE

Club Med's 70-acre (28 ha) resort of Turkoise, on Provo's northeast coast, overlooks a sweeping white-sand beach. One look at the breathtaking blue of the ocean is enough to explain the village's name—Turkoise. In contrast to the many arid stretches on the rest of the island, its grassy lawns are dotted with palm, coconut and fire trees. Lush, purple bougainvillea festoon the buildings of the village.

The entrance road, past the security booth, leads 200 yards (183 m) to the welcoming plaza at the center of the village.

The center includes a large swimming pool, the main restaurant and bar, the theater and the discotheque. It is also where the office, bank, telephone, mail boxes and message board are located.

The village is divided roughly in half. While facing the ocean the area on the right is called *Marina* and on the left side is *Florina*. Divers will prefer the *Marina* side where the scuba and snorkeling facilities are located. For wind surfers, sailors and tennis players the *Florina* side will be most convenient.

There are eight hard-surface tennis courts, four of which have lights for nighttime use. Rackets are available at the shack, while balls can be purchased at the boutique. There are also Ping-Pong tables.

Wind surfing and sailing can be found right on the beach. The water skiing dock is in the center of the village, in front of the swimming pool. No reservations are necessary. Just show up and take your turn as many times as you like.

An air-conditioned fitness center is near the theater; it is equipped with various exercise machines and free-weights.

Volleyball, basketball, soccer, touch football, softball and bocci games are played in the field near the center of the resort.

For the less athletically inclined, there is an arts and crafts shop with activities such as painting on silk and making costume jewelry.

The main restaurant serves breakfast, lunch and dinner buffet-style at tables for eight. There is a separate smoking section. For those who prefer to eat at odd hours, there are two annex restaurants, the Grill and the Pizzeria, at the end of *Florina*, near the tennis courts. One serves late breakfast and late lunch. At night the two restaurants offer a different fare. Tables are for two, four, six or large parties of 12 or

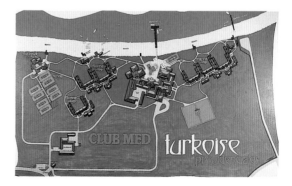

New Club Med regulations prohibit touching marine life. Nassau groupers often accompany divers and approach them closely.

more. There is no extra charge at these restaurants, but reservations are required.

The Grill, at dockside, features a nautical motif and offers a different menu each day. The Pizzeria is a relaxed, Italian-style eatery that features pasta and pizza as well as an antipasto buffet. Meals at both restaurants are served at your table.

The village has 600 beds. The air-conditioned rooms, in one- to three-story beach and garden front buildings, include private bathrooms with showers. All rooms are the same size, but some have king or oversize twin beds. Electronic safes and individual keys are standard. Each room has only one electrical outlet, plus a bathroom socket. There are also ice machines and a laundromat.

Children over 12 are allowed, but there are no special facilities for them; the village is mostly adult, singles and couples oriented.

Single rooms are available at extra charge, but there may be some restrictions during busy periods and holidays.

There are no telephones in the rooms; phones are available only in the village's main office. Arrangements for car rentals can be made there as well.

DIVING—A DEDICATED DIVE CENTER

Boats. The village has four dive vessels. They are the *High Rider*, a V-hull, 45-foot (14 m) that can accommodate up to 33 divers on two-tank dives; the *Santa Fe*, a 38-foot (12 m) V-hull designed to carry up to 26 divers on one- or two-tank trips; the 48-foot (15 m) *Abyss* that can carry up to 36 two-tank divers, and the *Miss Turkoise*, a 45-foot (14 m) pontoon boat with room for 40 divers on a two-tank expedition. The *Miss Turkoise* is usually used for local snorkeling trips.

Certification. PADI and NAUI open water and advanced certification is available. Most classes are held in the afternoon.

Equipment. Although guests are welcome to bring their own equipment, all diving necessities are available at the village. These include 80 cubic foot aluminum tanks, Scubapro buoyancy compensators, Scubapro G-200 regulators with gauges and octopus rigs, Beuchat graphite masks and fins, and weight belts. Halogen lights for night dives are also available free of charge, while full wet suits or shorties can be rented at daily or weekly rates. Aladin Pro wrist mounted dive computers are also available for rental.

Dive schedule. There are two morning dives a day and one night dive a week. For an extra fee, an additional dive can be arranged in the afternoon.

Facilities. The dive shack, on the *Marina* side, is a few yards from the beach, and includes a dock, fresh-water showers and secure storage rooms so dive gear does not have to be carried back and forth to guest rooms. The two Mako compressors are in a separate shack set back from the area to minimize noise.

Safety. All the dive boats are equipped with VHF radios, oxygen, decompression bars, first-aid kits and hookah regulators. In addition to having a physician skilled in treating diving related accidents at the village, all divemasters and instructors are trained in emergency first aid. There is a decompression chamber on Provo, a 10-minute drive from the village.

Non divers wishing to participate in dive training should bring a medical certification attesting to their physical fitness for diving.

Snorkeling. There are numerous snorkeling sites, especially inside the barrier reef, where coral heads in shallow water boast a profusion of multicolored barrel, tube and vase sponges. The reefs are also rich in brain, star and flower corals. Purple sea fans and gorgonians are common as well.

The most commonly seen fish at the snorkeling sites are queen angels, triggerfishes, wrasses, parrotfishes, butterflyfishes and schools of grunts. Occasionally seen are lobsters, turtles, nurse sharks and barracuda.

Visibility. Underwater visibility ranges from 50 to 100 feet (15-30 m), depending on sea conditions.

Water Temperature. The water is warmest during the summer months of July through September averaging between 80 and 82°F (27-28°C). During the fall and spring the temperature is usually between 77 and 80°F (25-27°C). In the winter the water may drop as low as 75°F (24°C) and not climb higher than 78°F (26°C).

Jojo, an Atlantic bottlenose dolphin, resides in the waters of Providenciales and playfully swims with one of the instructors.

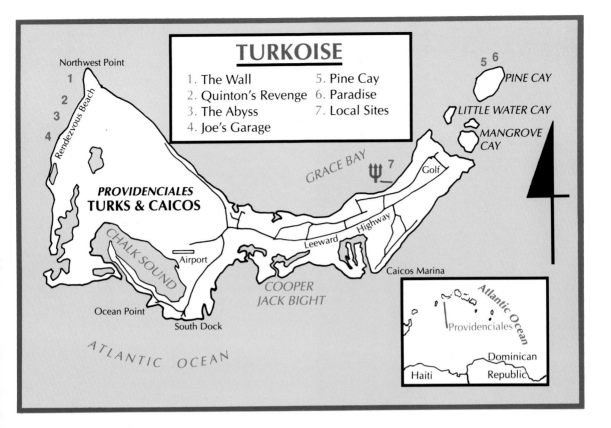

JOJO THE DOLPHIN

An Atlantic bottlenose dolphin known as JoJo has become something of a regular in the waters surrounding the Club Med village. Residents say he's been living in the shallow waters around Provo and Pine Cay since 1980, when he left the company of his brethren. He has a habit of sidling alongside swimmers and divers, and even tagging along with water skiers. JoJo has also been known to try stopping boats in search of playmates.

It is important to remember that JoJo is a wild animal. If you are lucky enough to meet up with JoJo, you should avoid swimming after him—a gesture he might interpret as a threat. Also you should not touch him, especially around his sensitive blow hole, as you could easily scare or anger him.

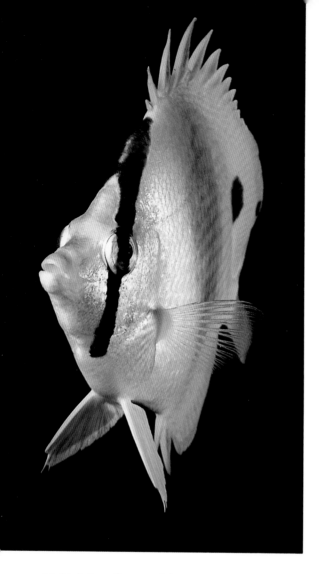

Night diving offers special opportunities for photographers because many fish, such as this spotfin butterflyfish, can be approached closely.

DIVE SITES

1. THE WALL

DEPTH:	60-130 FEET
	(18-39 M)
DISTANCE:	55 MINUTES

Boats visiting The Wall, Club Med's original offshore dive site for intermediate and advanced divers, generally moor about 100 yards (91 m) from the edge of the drop-off,

where the bottom is 45 to 50 feet (14-15 m) deep. A vast flat area of white sand dotted with coral heads, giant sea fans and yellow tube sponges leads to the drop-off. The uniform flatness of the approach can make finding the edge a little tricky, so it is recommended to fix your bearings topside. Noting the position of the sun relative to the wall is a good idea. If you are unsure of your direction stay close to the divemaster.

As divers approach the edge of the drop-off at 60 feet (18 m) the density of the coral formations increase until they become a solid conglomeration along the lip of the wall. Looking down into the depths, the water color changes dramatically to a deep blue. The most interesting area is between 70 and 100 feet (21-30 m). Here you will find many purple tube sponges on overhangs, while vase sponges sprout from uneven surfaces of the wall.

Most of the reef fish you will see, such as yellowtail jacks, squirrelfishes and Nassau groupers, prefer to roam the edge of the wall, but be sure to keep glancing into the open ocean. Jacks and other pelagics are frequently sighted cruising rapidly by. If you have a camera, be prepared for a quick shot.

Caution. As with any wall, especially in clear water, it is easy to drop too deep without realizing it. Be sure to watch your depth.

2. QUINTON'S REVENGE

DEPTH:	45-100+ FEET
	(14-30+ M)
DISTANCE:	60 MINUTES

Boats visiting this spot usually moor in 45 feet (14 m) of water, close to the edge of the wall. From the dive boat you can see the rich profusion of corals on the white sandy bottom. Usually you can drop right to the lip of the wall where the most interesting formations and marine life can be found. But there is plenty to see in the flats—brain corals with many colors of Christmas tree worms, pillar corals with polyps swaying in the gentle current, and star and finger corals in spectacular shapes and colors. Be sure to look for triggerfish and squirrelfishes hiding amongst the coral formations. Parrotfishes can often be seen (and heard) crunching on the coral with their hard beaks to extract the polyps. The rejected broken coral will become sand.

In the intensely blue water of the deep ocean off the wall, eagle rays are commonly seen, sometimes in groups of four or five. Blacktip sharks occasionally glide up from the depths for a curious look at the divers, but tend to keep their distance and rarely linger.

The best views of the wall are in the 100-foot (30 m) range where large purple tube sponges and gorgonians predominate, along with gaggles of yellowtails, Nassau groupers and trumpetfishes.

Be sure to watch your depth.

3. THE ABYSS

DEPTH:	55-130 FEET
	(17-39 M)
DISTANCE:	65 MINUTES

The chief characteristic of this site, after an approach over a bed of large purple sea fans and gorgonians, and schools of reef fish, is a vast vertical crevice in the wall that begins at 55 feet (17 m) and plunges to 120 (36 m). The crevice is hard to miss as it is located right off the edge when swimming out from the dive boat mooring. Swimming between the two huge colorful walls, amid schools of yellowtails and larger jacks, is a memorable experience.

Even in daylight, a dive light is handy for peering into the numerous cracks in the walls where you can often see red and white banded shrimp. At the bottom of the canyon, spider crabs and lobsters are abundant.

Photo tip. For a shot of a diver between the two walls try staying deep and shooting upwards.

Spider crabs leave their daytime crevices to forage for food at night.

There are many changes on the reef at night. Here a basket starfish, at the base of a sea fan, opens its lacy arms to feed on drifting plankton.

Underwater photographers capture a special moment as a three-foot (1 m) barracuda patiently hovers just above the reef at Joe's Garage.

4. JOE'S GARAGE

DEPTH:	80-100+ FEET
	(24-30+ M)
DISTANCE:	65 MINUTES

A cavern cutting about 25 feet (8 m) into the wall at a depth of 80 feet (24 m) is the highlight of this dive. The "garage" as it is called runs for at least a 100 feet (30 m). Its ceiling is encrusted with multicolored sponges, fan worms, feather dusters and many small anemones. Also found here are stinging hydroids, which, needless to say, should be kept at arm's length.

Photo tip. Photographers should enter the cavern first to get their shots, since exhaust bubbles from regulators can dislodge debris from the ceiling, ruining visibility.

Watch for a large, photogenic barracuda who has staked out part of this area. Schools of jacks are often visible at depths below 100 feet (30 m).

5. PINE CAY

DEPTH:	55-130+ FEET
	(17-39+ M)
DISTANCE:	45 MINUTES

This is an ideal dive for intermediate and advanced divers, especially those with cameras. The descent along the mooring line to the 55-foot (17 m) bottom offers views of a vast plateau blanketed with sea fans, pinnacles of pillar coral, massive brain coral and star coral. The visibility is usually good at this site and there is rarely any current. The vertical wall on the north side of this spot drops below 130 feet (39 m), so caution is advised.

The marine life here is especially rich and varied. Besides the usual reef fishes such as surgeonfishes, squirrelfishes, angelfishes, butterflyfishes, groupers and jacks, you can commonly see spotted eagle rays and schools of Atlantic spadefish.

6. PARADISE

DEPTH:	55-130 FEET
	(17-39 M)
DISTANCE:	45 MINUTES

Paradise is only a few minutes boat ride from Pine Cay and shares many similarities in topography and marine life. It is also home to several tame Nassau groupers, which loiter around the mooring line waiting hopefully for handouts. It is easy to tell that they have been fed in the past for they watch every move of your hands. These 30-pounders (14 kg) will stay a few inches (cm) from you, and if you reach into your vest pocket they will become very excited, moving their eyes and jostling for the closest position. You can hear the impact of their mouths as they push each other out of the way.

Photo tip. The yellow tube sponges and purple sea fans give the photographer nice backgrounds for photographing the groupers.

7. LOCAL SITES

DEPTH:	35-100+ FEET
	(11-30 M)
DISTANCE:	10-20 MINUTES

There are a large variety of local dive spots, beginning literally in front of the village just past the channel. Generally, the topography of each includes patches of white sand at a depth of 35 to 40 feet (11-12 m), with spines of coral leading north to the open sea. The depths along the lip of the wall average 55 to 60 feet (17-18 m). It drops to 100 to 140 feet (30-42 m) at the bottom.

Some sites feature specific curiosities. **Pinnacles** has tall columns of pillar coral and large, curious groupers. Numerous cave formations give **Cathedral** its name. **Grouper Hole** is home to numerous Nassau groupers who will follow you during your dive, and large schools of pesky yellowtails. At **Nurse Sharks** as the name suggests, nurse sharks are frequently seen in small caves of the reef formation.

Another popular site, **Fifi's Folly**, consists of dense concentrations of corals which form canyons leading toward the drop-off. Giant sea fans and star corals create a rewarding latticework of beauty for those divers who don't want to go much deeper than 50 feet (15 m).

CHAPTER **IV**   ST. LUCIA

West Indies

THE PAST

St. Lucia was once dubbed the "Helena" of the Caribbean for its captivating beauty. Nestled between Martinique 21 miles (34 km) to the north and St. Vincent 24 miles (39 km) to the south, the 27 by 14 mile (44-23 km) island straddles a volcanic ridge. Its lush landscape includes spectacular peaks, verdant valleys, rugged coastlines, luxurious beaches, and a simmering volcano.

Although Spain claimed the island in the 1500's, the first recorded European settlement was a colony of British subjects in 1638; they were wiped out three years later by the Carib Indians. The King of France claimed St. Lucia in 1642, and it became a part of the French West Indies until sold to M.M. Hoel and Du Parquet.

The French takeover ushered in a long period of fighting in which the settlers—mostly planters who had imported African slaves to work their plantations—first came under attack by the Indians and later by waves of rival British settlers. Before 1814, when it finally became a British Crown colony under the Treaty of Paris, St. Lucia changed hands 14 times.

It was granted full internal self-government in 1967, becoming a Commonwealth state in association with Britain, and in 1979 gained independence.

THE PRESENT

In spite of its British association there is a strong residual French influence, visible in some of the provincial-style architecture and those residents who speak a patois. The islanders are predominantly of mixed descent, a combination of white settlers, Africans brought to the islands as slaves, and Carib Indians. Most are Roman Catholic.

Derek Wolcott, the renowned Caribbean poet and playwright who won the 1992 Nobel Prize for Literature, was born in St. Lucia in 1930.

Although agriculture—chiefly bananas, cocoa and dairy products—has long been the backbone of the economy, there is a growing industrial and manufacturing sector. Tourism has emerged as one of the major sources of hard currency. However, the boom in hotel construction has caused some concern about its impact on the island's wildlife and delicate ecosystem. Much of the island's original rain forest has been destroyed over the last 20 years, which has landed the national bird, the St. Lucian parrot (*Amazona versicolor*), on the endangered species list.

Also foremost among the natural wonders of the island are its two most spectacular volcanic peaks, Gros Piton (2,619 feet [794 m]) and Petit Piton (2,461 feet [746 m]), thickly wooded spears rising out of the sea on the west coast. Not far away are the open vents and boiling sulphurous pools of Soufriere, known as the world's only "drive-through" volcano.

Children, as early as the age of four, have as much fun as mom and dad as they get to experience the thrill of breathing underwater one on one with an instructor.

Useful Information

Climate. The average temperature is about 79°F (26°C), but it can be cooler at higher elevations. Daytime highs can reach the high 80's F (30-32°C) with evenings usually in the mid-70's (24°C). The summer months are several degrees warmer than the winter months. The northeast trade winds make even the hottest days comfortable. The driest season is from January to April, August through October being the wettest months.

Currency. The East Caribbean Dollar is the legal currency. Travelers checks and major credit cards are accepted in most establishments.

Electricity. The voltage is 220 and the sockets are the large three blade sockets found in Britain making adapters and converters necessary. At the Club Med village there is a 110/220 outlet in the bathroom.

Entry and Exit Requirements. For American, Canadian and British citizens visas are not required for a stay less than six months. Adequate proof of identity such as a birth certificate or passport and a return ticket are required. Driver's licenses are not acceptable. There is a US$20.00 departure tax.

Etiquette. Lightweight clothing is appropriate year round. Swimming attire and short shorts should not be worn when in town or sightseeing. Topless bathing is not permitted.

Getting There. Saint Lucia has two airports. The one in the north of the island, next to the capitol of Castries, is called Vigie. The southern airport next to Vieux Fort is called Hewanorra Airport. American Airlines has service from San Juan to both airports and Club Med has its own weekly charters out of New York and Miami to Hewanorra Airport. British West Indies Airlines also has direct service from New York and Miami to the southern airport. Hewanorra Airport is about five minutes from the Club Med village, while Vigie is over an hour, so be sure to plan accordingly to avoid a lengthy and expensive taxi ride.

Language. English is the national language although you will also hear Creole spoken. French and English are used at the Club Med village.

Sightseeing. A good way to get an overview of the natural beauty of the island is to take a 20-minute helicopter ride offered by St. Lucia Helicopter (phone 453-6950) located in Castries. The helicopter can pick up passengers right from the Club Med landing pad. The ride will fly over the rain forest, volcano, the two Pitons and the highest peak on the island, Mt. Gimie (3,117 feet [945 m]). On a clear day you can see the islands of Martinique, St. Vincent, Dominica and Barbados.

The now dormant volcano of Soufriere with its sulphur scented steam and bubbling sulphur pools is an interesting place to visit. For a look at a picturesque fishing village, visit Soufriere which is close to the volcano and named for the sulphur smell prevalent in the area. Also close by are the Diamond Falls mineral baths whose waters are considered to be therapeutic. After visiting the baths you can stroll through the nearby botanical gardens. Another fun place to visit is the lively market in Castries, the island's capital.

Dining Outside Club Med

Kitmatrai   454-6328

Just a 10-minute taxi ride from the village, this reasonably-priced restaurant is situated on a hill overlooking a bay on St. Lucia's west coast. It has a local atmosphere with Caribbean decor and a lovely terrace. Specialties are Creole chicken and fish, lobster and local punch.

Il Piratta   454-6610

Italian specialties such as pasta, pizza and sea food are offered at this seaside restaurant located a 15-minute taxi ride from the village on the road north to the Pitons. Slightly more expensive than some other local restaurants, it is also a bit more sophisticated, but not so much that the local atmosphere is lost. There is no air-conditioning, however, the breeze coming off the ocean makes for comfortable dining.

Chak-Chak   454-6260

If you like Chinese food try this very affordable restaurant decorated oriental-style with bamboo and wood. It is in the center of the city of Vieux Fort, only a five-minute trip from the village. There is no air-conditioning and local atmosphere is guaranteed.

Club Med's St. Lucia facility is one of the Club's largest. Its 120 acres (49 ha) are located on the south of the island.

THE CLUB MED VILLAGE

This village, formerly the Halcyon Days Resort, was remodeled by Club Med and reopened in 1985. The dive center was added in 1989. The 120-acre (49 ha) site, on the southeast part of the island, is just a few minutes from Hewanorra Airport and Vieux Fort.

On entering the village, the golf practice range will be on your left and the hotel on your right. The welcome plaza leads to a large reception area of marble and pastel pinks, where you will find all offices and telephones (no telephones are available in the rooms). A few feet away are the boutique and the sea center where the diving lectures and dive sign-ups take place. The air-conditioned fitness center is also in this area. Facing the boutique is the theater where GO's will have nightly presentations. Continuing along the hallway will take you to the large swimming pool, the bar area and a narrow beach.

This village is spread out, offering a lot of open space for walking. Many lawns, purple bougainvillea and large quantities of coconut trees give the village a lush tropical flavor.

The two wings of the hotel are named Vieux Fort and Castries. All rooms are identical in the four-story building and have air-conditioning with private balconies facing the ocean. Double occupancy rooms with two twin beds, connecting rooms and single rooms are subject to availability. There is an extra charge for single rooms.

The main restaurant is upstairs above the reception area and serves buffet breakfast, lunch and dinner at tables for eight. There is a separate smoking section. Two annex restaurants give you other options for dining. The Club House, which serves French cuisine, offers late breakfast, late lunch and dinner served at your table. Tables for two are available. There is no additional charge, but reservations are required for dinner. The second annex, Cadi's Pub, offers the same service, but serves American food.

St. Lucia is recommended for children. About 200 yards (182 m) from the village center is the Mini Club for children ages 2 through 11. It has its own swimming pool, and offers horseback and pony riding, and go-cart racing. Another highlight is the circus school.

Adults may also enjoy horseback riding, golf, archery or tennis on one of the eight composition courts which are all lit at night. They can also use the fitness center and the circus school. This area has some excellent wind surfing, which takes place just a few minutes walk along the beach. There is a shuttle to the wind surfing shack as well.

DIVING—A DEDICATED DIVE CENTER

Boats. The village has two scuba boats. One is the 55-foot (17 m) *Blue Lagoon*, which has a cruising speed of 15 knots and can carry 40 divers for two-tank dives. There is a water cooled compressor on board. The *Long John* is 52 feet (16 m), with a double deck and a cruising speed of 14 knots. It can carry up to 45 divers on two-tank dives and also has a water cooled compressor on board. There is also a snorkeling boat.

Certification. Both NAUI and PADI open water and advanced courses are available as is the Club Med resort course. Most courses take place in the afternoon.

Equipment. Aluminum 80 cubic foot tanks, Scubapro buoyancy jackets, and Scubapro G-200 regulators with gauges and octopus rigs, are standard equipment. Masks and fins are Beuchat. Lights are provided for night dives. Wet suits and Aladin Pro computers can be rented on a daily or weekly basis. Tanks remain on board the boats.

Dive Schedule. There are two dives a day with one night dive per week. Divers have a choice of one- or two-tank dives with one boat leaving at 8:00 A.M. and the second one at 8:30 A.M. For an extra fee a third dive in the afternoon is often available.

Facilities. There are two locations used for scuba activities. The sea center located next to the boutique in the village center is the meeting point for sign ups, lectures, classroom instruction, and video watching. The scuba shack is the pickup area for equipment and the meeting point for dive trips. It is near the welcome plaza at the entrance of the hotel. Gear storage and rinse buckets are available. A

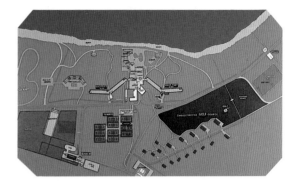

dive bag is also provided. A bus picks up the divers at the dive shack for the 10-minute trip to the dive boats on the other side of the island.

Mini Club. Twice a week in the pool there is an introduction to breathing underwater with scuba for children ages 4 through 12. They are outfitted with pony bottles and a diving instructor swims next to them, maintaining contact. This is not "scuba training" and the children are in only several feet of water under direct supervision. Twelve is the minimum age for scuba certification.

Safety. Oxygen and first aid equipment are on board the dive boats, and the instructors and divemasters are trained in emergency first aid procedures for diving and other injuries. A doctor knowledgeable about scuba injuries, and two nurses are in the village. The nearest recompression chamber is in Fort de France.

Snorkeling. The snorkeling boat goes out every day at 10 A.M. on local snorkel trips. Twice a week there is a snorkeling picnic which goes to the Pitons. It leaves at 10 A.M., returns at 5 P.M. and serves a barbecue lunch on board. In the clear, shallow water of the Pitons area there are many corals, sea fans, large barrel and azure vase sponges, trumpetfishes, parrotfishes, sergeant majors, and goatfishes.

Visibility. Visibility ranges from 50 to well over 100 feet (15-30 m) depending on sea conditions.

Water Temperature. In January the water can drop to as low as 75°F (24°C), but from April through October it can reach as high as 82°F (28°C). Lows during the summer are generally at least 80°F (27°C).

ST. LUCIA

DIVE SITES

8. *LESLEEN M*

DEPTH:	35-65 FEET
	(11-20 M)
DISTANCE:	90 MINUTES
CURRENT:	OFTEN STRONG

The 160-foot (48 m) freighter, *Lesleen M* was sunk in 1986 as part of an artificial reef program. She sits upright and intact in an area of white sand, and on a clear day you can see the wreck from the surface as the top is only 35 feet (11 m) deep. This is the furthest dive site from the dock so it is usually a one-tank dive.

The mooring line is attached to the wreck. Because of the often present current you should descend on the line so you won't get swept away from the wreck. The hatches and cables were removed before sinking so it is an easy wreck to penetrate.

A healthy growth of gorgonians, colorful hydroids and sponges now covers the wreck,

As part of St. Lucia's artificial reef program, the Lesleen M was sunk in 1986 and is now home to some of the Caribbean's most interesting underwater life.

Most dives on St. Lucia are drift dives because the wall is so close to the cliff it prevents mooring. The boat drops off the divers and picks them up as they surface.

especially along the hull. There is an abundant variety of invertebrates hiding among the many crevices of the wreck and along the many corridors.

Photo tip. With visibility generally over 100 feet (30 m) you can often see the whole length of the wreck, so wide-angle shots are appropriate. Divers swimming through the interior corridors offer good shooting opportunities, but one of the best backdrops is the propeller. If you pay close attention you may get to observe sea horses that frequent this area of the wreck.

9. DEVIL'S DROP

DEPTH:	35-130+ FEET
	(11-39+ M)
DISTANCE:	70 MINUTES
CURRENT:	OFTEN STRONG

As with most of the dive sites in St. Lucia, this is a drift dive. The boat will drop you off and pick you up when you surface at the end of the dive. It is required on this dive that the group follow a scuba instructor equipped with a float.

The dive begins in 35 feet (11 m) of water where the current is not too strong. As you approach the wall, which begins at a depth of 40 feet (12 m) the current generally increases. The most attractive section of the wall is between 40 and 60 feet (12-18 m). Here you will encounter many azure vase sponges that appear almost phosphorescent. Yellow tube and giant barrel sponges surrounded by chromis and wrasses can also be seen along the wall. Pelagics, such as jacks and bonitos, are regularly viewed in the deep blue water seaward of the wall. Visibility is usually excellent.

Photo tip. The masses of different varieties of sponges intermingled with red gorgonians can make it difficult for photographers to select their shots, especially when drifting by in the current. Most likely you will get one shot at a subject. By the time your strobe has recycled you will have drifted on. Using models is also difficult under these conditions and requires a great deal of planning before the dive.

10. TEQUILA SUNRISE

DEPTH:	30-100 FEET
	(9-30 M)
DISTANCE:	70 MINUTES

Although close to Devil's Drop, this site is more protected so there is less current. The wall here is not as steep as Devil's Drop, but the same section, between 40 and 60 feet (12-18 m) is the most interesting. Visibility is usually over 100 feet (30 m) allowing you to see the boat on the surface as it follows the divers.

In areas as small as 20 square feet (1.86 ca) it is common to be able to count over 10 varieties of coral and numerous colorful sponges. Finger, brain, star, cactus, sheet and leaf are some of the more prominent corals. Between the masses of coral are sand flats where you can usually see lizardfishes with their heads popping out of the sand. Pay attention to the little alcoves and crevices in the coral formations. White spotted spiny lobsters, spider crabs and other invertebrates are often seen tucked in their recesses.

11. THE ARCH

DEPTH:	15-80 FEET
	(5-24 M)
DISTANCE:	65 MINUTES

This is one of the only dives with a mooring. Since the site is inside a protected bay there is no current and the visibility of up to 100 feet (30 m) will give beginning divers a chance for a long, leisurely dive. There are many interesting things to see in the shallow water. You can swim through a coral archway by the mooring, for example, which is only 25 feet (8 m) deep. The arch is surrounded by an impressive amount of yellow and green sea fans.

Red encrusting sponges growing on the big boulders add splashes of color to this largely green environment. Also in the shallow water are abundant brown and blue chromis as well as yellowhead and bluehead wrasse.

If you decide to drop to the 30- to 50-foot (9-15 m) depth level, the topography changes as the slope slowly descends. Between the masses of sheet, leaf and brain corals are sandy sections where there are large populations of sharptail eels. They are more easily viewed at night when they swim in the open water foraging for food. Fortunately, this is one of the sites commonly used for the weekly night dive.

12. FANTASIA

DEPTH:	30-80 FEET
	(9-24 M)
DISTANCE:	65 MINUTES

This is another site that can be dived at two different depth levels. In the shallow 30-foot (9 m) range, buttresses of coral and rock formations jut perpendicular to the deeper water and are separated by channels of sand. Sea fans, anemones and hydroids grow from the formations. Christmas tree worms unfold from the encrusting leaf coral, retracting almost instantly at the slightest indication of shadows or disturbances in the water. Approach them cautiously and you will be treated to a myriad of colors. Arrow crabs and cleaner shrimp can also be seen.

One of the highlights of deeper depths is a vast section of yellowfinger coral where large numbers of chromis find sanctuary. This well protected spot is also used for night diving.

Photo tip. Cameras are best equipped with a close-up lens for the shallow portions of this site.

13. KEYHOLE PINNACLES

DEPTH:	6-90 FEET
	(2-27 M)
DISTANCE:	60 MINUTES
LEVEL:	INTERMEDIATE TO
	ADVANCED
CURRENT:	OFTEN STRONG

This site, north of Soufriere Bay, is easy to spot because of a sharp rock rising from the water. Underwater, the topography is extremely unusual and very different from other sites. Four cone-shaped pinnacles rise from the 90-foot (27 m) bottom, one of them coming to within 6 feet (2 m) of the surface. They are covered with red and white gorgonians, and many sea fans. The sides and bottoms of the pinnacles are decorated with large brown vase sponges. Swimming between these pinnacles is like being in a large canyon. Current can be strong here as can surge because of the turbulence created by the pinnacles.

Photo tip. This is an excellent spot for wide-angle photography.

An encounter with the long-armed lobster occurs only at night. During the day, this bright red crustacean lives deep in caves and is rarely seen.

Breathtaking from above and below, the Two Pitons tower over the waters containing most of St. Lucia's dive sites. This is also a good place for hiking.

14. PITON WALL

DEPTH:	50-130+ FEET (15-39+ M)
DISTANCE:	55-60 MINUTES
CURRENT:	OFTEN STRONG

Located at the foot of the smallest of the two Pitons, this drift dive is known for its vertical wall starting at 50 feet (15 m) and dropping to well beyond sport diving limits. Not all sections of this wall are perfectly vertical, but the angle remains very steep.

Colorful barrel and vase sponges, and a multitude of corals such as brain and leaf carpet the wall. Check all the small crevices for invertebrates and squirrelfishes. In the intense blue water seaward of the wall schools of cruising jacks and turtles are often seen.

Caution. Be sure to check your depth often. Because of the clarity of the water you may not realize your depth. The current can also be strong at this spot.

15. BLACK FOREST

DEPTH:	25-75 FEET (8-23 M)
DISTANCE:	55 MINUTES
LEVEL:	INTERMEDIATE

A profusion of gorgonians give Black Forest its name. The gorgonians can be found at about 70 feet (21 m). They are actually red, but because of the absorption of color they appear black. Careful observation among the

Large groups of barrel sponges can be found in St. Lucia's clear blue waters. Growing only one-half inch (12 cm) a year, they can live for more than a century.

gorgonian stalks may reveal slender filefishes. Other marine life found here are arrow crabs, spotted cleaning shrimps, flamingo tongue cowries, pipefish and spotted drums.

Parrotfishes decorated with numerous patterns and colors are abundant in this huge reservoir of food. They are very interesting to watch as they noisily munch coral, eating the polyps and spitting out the broken bits of coral.

Look for peacock flounders which can often be approached to within a few inches (cm) as they lay on the small sand flats between the coral, trusting their almost perfect camouflage for protection.

16. STEVO'S PLAYGROUND

DEPTH:	25-60 FEET
	(8-18 M)
DISTANCE:	55 MINUTES
CURRENT:	OFTEN STRONG

This spot, close to the point of Gros Piton, is another drift dive as the current is often strong.

At the beginning of the dive the bottom is sandy and interspersed with mushroom-shaped blocks of coral. The bottom slopes gradually seaward. Even with the current, because of the gradual slope this dive is appropriate for all levels of divers.

The most interesting depth is about 50 feet (15 m) where divers will find an abundance and diversity of marine life, especially surgeonfishes and parrotfishes. There are lots of honeycomb cowfish and smooth trunkfish, which because they are slow swimmers, can be approached very closely. There are also porcupinefish here. While they are fun to swim with please don't touch or frighten them as it is only when scared that they puff up with water.

Look for trumpetfishes hovering vertically among the gorgonians, and an occasional sea horse. Scorpionfish are common at this site, but because they are so well camouflaged it takes a really sharp eye to spot them.

Beautiful purple vase sponges, commonly seen in Caribbean waters, accent St. Lucia's reefs.

CHAPTER V   COLUMBUS ISLE

Bahamas

THE PAST

The island of San Salvador in the Bahamas is thought by many historians to be where Columbus first set foot in the New World in 1492. In any case it wasn't until 1640 that a permanent settlement was established on the island by Puritans—most from Bermuda—fleeing religious persecution.

Originally called Guanahani by the native Lucayan Indians, the island was later named Watling's Island by the British Government after a noted buccaneer, Captain George Watling, who is said to have visited the island frequently. In 1926, the legislature formally changed its name back to San Salvador, which is what Columbus christened the island where he made his first landfall.

THE PRESENT

Today a large, simple white cross surrounded by flags marks the spot on Long Bay where Columbus may have stepped ashore.

San Salvador is about 12 miles (19 km) long and seven miles (11 km) wide, and is located almost 200 miles (323 km) southeast of Nassau, the capital of the Bahamas. Vegetation is limited to small trees and bushes, and nowhere does the elevation exceed 100 feet (30 m) above sea level. The main attraction is the miles of magnificent white sand beaches that line the perimeter of the island.

Approximately 600 people live on San Salvador in small scattered settlements. The most prominent town is Cockburn Town where the island's commissioner resides. It consists of only one street with its houses and shops clustered around an Anglican and a Catholic church.

San Salvador is largely undeveloped. Until Club Med opened its Columbus Isle village in December 1992, the only resort on the island was the 20-room Riding Rock Inn, which has been catering to divers since 1974.

USEFUL INFORMATION

Climate. Highs during the winter months reach about 79°F (26°C), dropping to a low of about 64°F (18°C) overnight. Daytime highs hover close to 90°F (32°C) in the summer, while overnight lows are in the mid-70's F (23-24°C).

Currency. The Bahamian dollar, which is equal in value to the U.S. dollar, is the official currency, but U.S. dollars are also accepted, as are major credit cards. Collectors and non-collectors alike will find Bahamian currency interesting with its $3 bill, square 15 cent pieces and fluted 10 cent pieces.

Electricity. Standard voltage is 110 volts with U.S. type outlets.

Entry and Exit Requirements. Citizens of the United States, Canada, the United Kingdom and Commonwealth States do not need passports, as long as the visit does not exceed three weeks. Adequate identification such as a birth certificate is required as is a return ticket. Driver's licenses are not accepted as identification. There is a $13.00 departure tax, but children under the age of 3 years are exempt.

Etiquette. The people of the islands are friendly and helpful. If the service seems unhurried at times, the relaxed and casual pace can help you unwind. The dress code is informal, but topless sunbathing is not permitted. Preservation of the environment—underwater and topside—is a major priority on San Salvador.

Swimming side by side with a large Nassau grouper adds a special touch to any dive.

Getting There. With the opening of the Club Med village American Airlines began turbo-prop charter service three times a week from Miami to the Cockburn Town Airport. Once a week Paradise Island Airlines also flies from Miami, while Bahamas Air has flights four times a week from Nassau with a stopover on Cat Island. Currently the airstrip is not long enough to handle jets. The Club Med village is only a few minutes drive from the airport.

Language. English is the national language with English and French spoken at the Club.

Sightseeing. For a look at plantation life in the early 1800's visit Farquharson's Plantation known locally as Blackbeard's Castle. The substantial ruins include what appear to be the main house, a prison and a kitchen. There is also an unusual cattle trough cut from solid rock. The owner of the plantation was Charles Farquharson, the Justice of the Peace for Watling's Island. The journal he kept for the year 1831-32 is perhaps the only surviving firsthand account of plantation life on the island.

Another plantation, Watling's Castle (or Sandy Point Estate), is at the south end of the island overlooking French Bay. The ruins are of a late 18th century loyalist plantation house.

An interesting stop is at the hand-operated Dixon Hill Lighthouse, built by the Imperial Lighthouse Service. It has a visibility of 90 miles (145 km) and projects 4,000 candlepower, and is one of only 10 kerosene lighthouses in the world, four of which are in the Bahamas.

Ten minutes south of the Club Med village is the Columbus Monument, the white cross marking the spot where he may have landed. There is also a replica of an Indian village designed to appear as it may have when Columbus arrived. Next to the monument is the large bronze bowl which held the Olympic flame when it traveled from Greece to the 1968 Olympics in Mexico City.

DINING OUTSIDE OF CLUB MED

The Riding Rock   VHF Channel 6

Located in the Riding Rock Inn, this restaurant with a friendly, island atmosphere has a terrace view of the Caribbean. Specialties are American and Bahamian dishes of rice and chicken, fresh seafood, spicy conch chowder and fresh home baked bread. Also visit the cozy Driftwood Bar adjacent to the restaurant. It is decorated with artifacts from local shipwrecks and dedications from previous visitors either engraved on the bar or written on t-shirts and hung up for all to see. It is within walking distance of the Club Med village. Prices are moderate to expensive.

Three Ships   VHF Channel 6

There are no decorations at Three Ships located in Cockburn Town, but the food is good. The fare consists of pork chops, chicken, conch, or fish. Reservations are necessary and you need to order your meal when making reservations. They can be reached via radio on Channel 6 since they have no phone. Prices are moderate.

THE CLUB MED VILLAGE

The village was named Columbus Isle because the 1992 opening coincided with the 500th anniversary of Christopher Columbus's first landing in the New World, possibly on this island. In Columbus' honor, the sun, moon and stars, by which he navigated, are the major design elements used throughout the village.

Situated on 80 acres (32 ha), the village is located on the 3 1/2 mile (5.6 km) crescent beach of Bonefish Bay along the island's northwest coast. The dunes and the seashore are protected from erosion by wild plants such as sea oats, sea grapes and dwarf palms.

Located at the center of the village are the swimming pool, outside and inside bar, lounge, boutique and offices. Nightly entertainment is held in the covered open-air theater/dance floor behind the bar. Lush tropical greenery, colorful bougainvillea and dipladenia accent the village throughout.

Adjacent to this area is the air-conditioned main dining room decorated in classic Bahamian style with whitewashed teak chairs and tables, and stucco walls. Breakfast, lunch and dinner are served buffet style with a wide variety of Bahamian and international specialties. For more intimate dining the village also features two annex restaurants located near the dive center on the southern point of the village.

Besides scuba diving, activities available are sailing (hobie cats and lasers), wind surfing,

The Columbus Isle village, which opened in 1992, offers sparkling turquoise waters and miles of sandy beaches.

kayaking, water skiing, snorkeling, water exercise, aerobics, tennis (10 courts, three lit for night play), soccer, baseball, basketball and for an extra fee deep-sea fishing.

Covered walkways lead from the village center to the accommodations, which are in two-story clusters of bungalows, painted in vibrant tones of yellow, green, blue or red with white gingerbread wood trim. Each cluster contains four spacious rooms all of which have wall-to-ceiling glass doors leading to a private balcony or patio overlooking the Caribbean.

Unlike most other Club Med resorts there are telephones, televisions and mini-refrigerators in the rooms. There is a choice of either queen or twin beds. Single rooms should be requested when making reservations, and are subject to availability and an extra charge. The village is designed for 520 guests.

Coin-operated washers and dryers, irons and ironing boards are available.

The village is recommended for guests 12 years and older as there are no special facilities for children.

THE SUN, MOON AND STARS

This village was opened on the 500th anniversary of Columbus's landing in the new world and the Club's interior designer, Gisela Trigano, wanted the village to honor Columbus in an unusual way.

The unifying theme is the sun, moon and stars—the celestial bodies used for navigation by Columbus and other great explorers. Even the door knobs are engraved with a sun or moon. Throughout the village are paintings and artifacts from far away places visited by these early explorers. For more than two years, Ms. Trigano and a team of architects collected these treasures from Africa, India, Sumatra, Thailand, China, Burma, Indonesia, New Guinea, Brazil and Peru.

DIVING—A DEDICATED DIVE CENTER

Boats. The *Blue Manta* and *Stingray* are two specially designed 48-foot (15 m) catamarans that cruise at 13 knots. Their wide 25-foot (8 m) beams contribute to a comfortable and spacious ride for up to 45 divers on two-tank dives. The identical boats have a large upper deck for sunbathing and ample benches for seating. Two large ladders and a dive platform make entering and exiting the water easy.

Certification. PADI and NAUI open water and advanced certification is available with a small charge for books. The Club Med resort course is offered free.

Equipment. The dive center is equipped with aluminum tanks (80's) in a color-coded system; yellow for instructors, white for safety, and guests have blue tanks for the first dive and pink for the second. Scubapro buoyancy compensators and R-190 regulators with octopus rigs are standard equipment. Fins and masks are made by Beuchat. Henderson wet suits and Aladin Pro computers are available for rent.

Dive Schedule. Certified divers can make two morning dives a day. There is an additional dive in the afternoon available for an extra fee. Once a week there is a night dive.

Facilities. The dive shack is part of a large building housing the infirmary, recompression chamber, doctor's office, conference room, and on the second floor, the two annex restaurants. A large room offers individual space for storing dive gear. Rinse tanks and fresh water showers are available as well. Two Mako compressors fill the tanks on the boats via a high pressure line to the dock.

Safety. The village has its own recompression chamber and a trained scuba doctor on site. Dive instructors and divemasters are trained in first aid for scuba related and other injuries. There are first aid kits, oxygen and VHF radios on board each boat. Decompression bars are hung 15 feet (5 m) deep on either side of the boats during dives and are equipped with hookah regulators for emergency air. An inflatable safety boat is on board each dive boat for emergency evacuation.

Snorkeling. A third 48-foot (15 m) catamaran, identical with the scuba boats takes up to 50 snorkelers to a variety of places, most of which are about a 10-minute ride from the village. The shallow water ranging from 10 to 25 feet (3-8 m) is extremely clear at most of these sites. The coral patches interspersed with white sand patches are abundant with marine life. Clusters of elkhorn coral thrive on top of the reef. Schooling grunts, goatfishes foraging in the sand and parrotfishes crunching coral are commonly seen occurrences. Snappers, groupers, and butterflyfishes also inhabit the surroundings. Out on the sandy bottom stingrays are often seen.

Visibility. Visibility is usually excellent, ranging from 100 to 150 feet (45 m), except during turbulent conditions.

Water Temperature. During the winter months the water temperature can drop as low as 71°F (22°C), but usually averages in the mid-70's F (23-24°C). In the summer the temperature is generally between 80 and 82°F (27-28°C).

With its 25-foot (8 m) beam and 48-foot (15 m) length, the catamaran Blue Manta *provides a spacious and stable platform for divers. It cruises at 14 knots and can carry as many as 45 divers on a two-tank dive.*

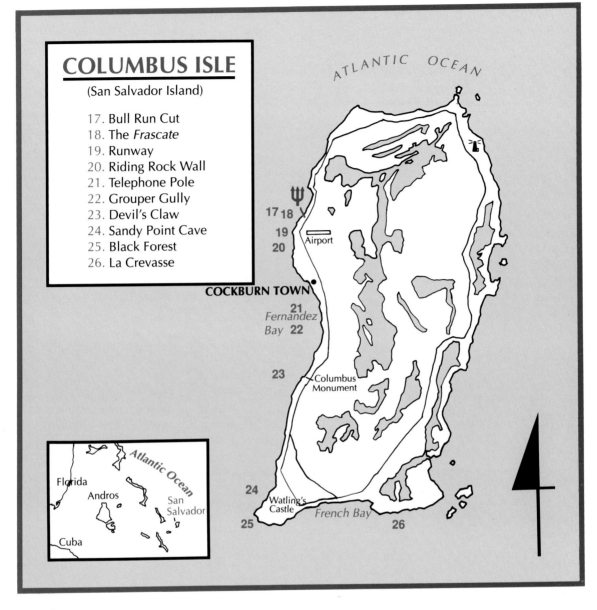

COLUMBUS ISLE

(San Salvador Island)

17. Bull Run Cut
18. The *Frascate*
19. Runway
20. Riding Rock Wall
21. Telephone Pole
22. Grouper Gully
23. Devil's Claw
24. Sandy Point Cave
25. Black Forest
26. La Crevasse

ATLANTIC OCEAN

17 18
19
20 Airport

COCKBURN TOWN

21
Fernandez
Bay 22

23 Columbus
Monument

24
Watling's
Castle French Bay
25 26

Atlantic Ocean
Florida
Andros
San
Salvador
Cuba

DIVE SITES

17. BULL RUN CUT

DEPTH:	35-100 FEET
	(11-30 M)
DISTANCE:	5 MINUTES

This convenient wall dive is right past the cut in the reef in front of the Club Med village. The dive starts at 35 feet (11 m) where there are canyons running through the coral heading towards the wall. In this shallow area are some massive specimens of elkhorn coral, which offer shelter to schools of damselfishes.

When you reach the drop-off you can't help but notice the intense blue water of the deep ocean. The wall drops to a small plateau at 80 feet (24 m) before continuing into deeper water. A large tunnel big enough for groups of divers to pass through is in the 80-90-foot (24-27 m) range. There are many more barrel sponges growing from small platforms on the wall at this spot than there are at the southern dive sites. You will also encounter more invertebrates such as lobsters and crabs which seem to favor the sanctuary of the numerous caverns and crevices in the coral.

18. THE *FRASCATE*

DEPTH:	15-20 FEET
	(5-6 M)
DISTANCE:	5 MINUTES

The wreck of the island freighter *Frascate* is right in front of the village. On New Year's Day 1902 the 261-foot (79 m) steel ship ran aground on the reef. During World War I, the wreck was deemed a navigational hazard and blown apart by the military.

Today the encrusted wreckage remains scattered among the coral. Fire coral is especially prevalent, so to be on the safe side practice good buoyancy control and avoid brushing against anything.

The large boilers are the easiest part of the wreck to spot and are big enough that divers can swim into them. The engine shaft, anchor chain and winches are also recognizable among the remains. Shipwrecks always make a dramatic background for photographs and this wreck is no exception.

Small black durgon are abundant here. In addition, tiger groupers, queen triggers and goatfishes all find refuge around the wreckage. Moray eels can usually be seen lurking in holes, if you look carefully. Small multicolored Christmas tree worms abound on tops of many small coral heads.

For those interested in a more streamlined approach, Columbus Isle provides a unique specialty course—kayak diving!

19. RUNWAY

DEPTH:	35-100+ FEET
	(11-30+M)
DISTANCE:	5-10 MINUTES
LEVEL:	INTERMEDIATE TO
	ADVANCED
CURRENT:	OFTEN STRONG

Three hundred yards (273 m) offshore from the end of the airport runway the reef drops in a straight wall. Inside the reef is a protected area between 35 to 45 feet (11-14 m) deep which makes an excellent night dive. In this shallow area the sandy bottom is scattered with small to large mounds of coral covered with sea fans, sea whips and numerous marine creatures such as arrow crabs and flame scallops. Loggerhead and blackball sponges are commonly found in this area.

Continuing over the reef, you will come to large masses of corals on the lip where the wall begins to slope steeply. There are some small cuts through the coral and several small caverns. Large schools of Bermuda chub and grunts will accompany your progress down the slope. The wall slopes until 60 feet (18 m) where there is a vertical drop-off. As you hang over the deep blue of the open ocean and glide along the wall, you will see large clusters of purple tube sponges. Elephant ear and finger sponges also festoon the wall. Sea turtles are often seen here as well.

20. RIDING ROCK WALL

DEPTH:	35-100 FEET
	(11-30 M)
DISTANCE:	10 MINUTES

A series of coral ridges spaced by sandy canyons are found at this site in front of the Riding Rock Inn. The coral rises from the 50-foot (15 m) bottom to within 35 feet (11 m) of the surface.

The vertical wall drops to about 80 feet (24 m) where the bottom continues sloping to 100 feet (30 m) before dropping into depths beyond scuba limits. Two deep, narrow crevices house large Nassau groupers and big crabs. Colorful encrusting sponges, orange ball anemones, scorpion fish and spotted morays are most commonly seen here.

This is a good site for night dives. At night the beam of your light will bring out even more colors, and there is a good chance of seeing an octopus changing its color pattern as it moves from one area to another. Close attention to the bottom will reveal many small invertebrates such as banded coral shrimp and arrow crabs.

21. TELEPHONE POLE

DEPTH:	40-130+ FEET
	(12-39+ M)
DISTANCE:	15 MINUTES

Telephone Pole is located right next to Cathedral and is aptly named for the wooden telephone pole lying on the bottom. The wall begins at 40 feet (12 m) and drops to depths greater than 130 feet (39 m).

When you come to the telephone pole on the sandy flats before the drop-off, follow the direction it points. It will aim you to a cut through the wall. Before going all the way through the wall the cut turns into a tunnel which exits the wall at a depth of about 80 feet (24 m). Swimming to the end of the tunnel will give you a fabulous window of cobalt blue water.

On the lip of the wall, friendly groupers that were fed in the past approach divers closely looking for a handout. An unusual sight here is a friendly jack fish which rivals the groupers in seeking attention. Being an open water species, jacks usually keep their distance from divers. While making your safety stop, keep your eyes on the edge of the wall. Many divers have seen hammerhead sharks cruising by.

This is an excellent site for photographers and for observing fish behavior. There is usually no current and visibility often exceeds 150 feet (45 m).

Colorful sponges and gorgonians adorn the walls of San Salvador. Keep your eyes open for large pelagics in the deep blue waters seaward of the walls.

Large cuts in the reef at depths of less than 80 feet (24 m) are typical of the underwater topography of San Salvador.

22. GROUPER GULLY

DEPTH:	40-120 FEET
	(12-36 M)
DISTANCE:	15 MINUTES

Continuing south will bring you to Grouper Gully another site with unique characteristics. The gully is actually a small cut that goes through the wall. On both sides of the cut are a series of small caverns. The descent is gradual and starts at 40 feet (12 m) with small plateaus at 60 and 80 feet (18-24 m).

The many Nassau groupers in the gully will come right up to divers. For photographers this can even be an inconvenience as the groupers will put their mouths a few inches from the camera lens. Most likely they are observing their reflection, but until they move further away you can't shoot.

If you want to feed the groupers, ask your dive guide for advice. Remember you should feed only products from the sea. Avoid cheese, crackers or anything else that is not part of the grouper's normal diet.

23. DEVIL'S CLAW

DEPTH:	45-90 FEET
	(14-27 M)
DISTANCE:	20 MINUTES
LEVEL:	INTERMEDIATE TO
	ADVANCED

The wall at this site faces to the north which makes the lighting very different from the previous sites. The sun shines on the inside of the reef and the lip of the drop-off, but leaves the wall in shadow.

There are three deep cuts in the face of the wall beginning at 45 feet (14 m), big enough for divers to swim through. The wall drops vertically to 90 feet (27 m) where there is a small plateau before continuing to descend gradually in an undulating fashion. At the end of the cuts is a cavern which provides shelter for jacks and barracuda.

The most interesting sights are in the 90-foot (27 m) range. The large coral heads seen in deep water from the plateau may tempt you, but they are actually at a depth greater than 150 feet (45 m)! Plate coral, hanging rope sponges and black coral are the prominent features of the deep portion of the wall and reef.

The usual Nassau groupers and schools of grunts can be seen here along with an occasional king mackerel. Visibility generally ranges from 100 to 150 feet (30-45 m).

Photo tip. Because of the angle of the sun, this is a good spot to shoot classic silhouette shots of divers. Position your model about 30 feet (9 m) above you and shoot upwards using the sun as a background.

24. SANDY POINT CAVE

DEPTH:	25-125 FEET
	(8-38 M)
DISTANCE:	25 MINUTES
LEVEL:	INTERMEDIATE TO
	ADVANCED

The mooring for this dive is next to a large sand hole by the southern point of the island. The top of the wall is at a depth of only 25 feet (8 m).

Follow the large cut through the wall which will bring you to a depth of 50 feet (15 m). Drop down the wall to 100 feet (30 m) and then turn to your right (the open water will be to your left). Swim along the wall until you come to another cut that will bring you to a large cavern. There are several openings to the cavern in the 90-foot (27 m) range. An uncommonly large barrel sponge about six feet (2 m) in diameter is outside the largest opening. Encrusting sponges carpet the cavern's interior.

The wall itself is covered with clumps of black coral and purple tube sponges. There are many large and colorful sponges throughout this site, which is excellent for wide-angle photography. The visibility is usually very good except during a strong outgoing tide when sand can be swept from the channels into the water column.

25. BLACK FOREST

DEPTH:	40-130+ FEET
	(12-39+ M)
DISTANCE:	25 MINUTES
LEVEL:	ADVANCED
CURRENT:	OFTEN STRONG

Continuing along the shoreline, the wall gets increasingly vertical and closer to the shore. Below the mooring is a wide sand flat that is funneled to a cut in the wall.

Dropping over the lip of the wall will reveal an abundance of vase, tube and rope sponges along with gorgonians and black coral. Keep your dive at the 100-foot (30 m) level where the most interesting marine life can be found. Be careful not to get so distracted by the beauty of the wall that you forget to watch your depth. It is easy to inadvertently drop well below scuba limits here.

At a depth of 100 feet (30 m), turn left (the open water will be on your right) and swim along the wall until you come to a large cut. This area is like a piece of Swiss cheese, riddled with holes and caverns, many of them connected to each other. Work your way upward exploring the many tunnels as you go. It is useful to have a dive light to view the darkened interiors of the many crevices.

Unfortunately, this little paradise is not well protected and therefore not accessible at all times. Conditions are ideal when the wind is blowing north or northwest.

26. LA CREVASSE

DEPTH:	30-130 FEET
	(9-39 M)
DISTANCE:	45 MINUTES
CURRENT:	OFTEN STRONG

This dive site, where the cliffs lining the shore are only 100 yards (91 m) from the mooring, is the furthest spot from the village.

There are three different sections of this dive making it a good spot for both novice and advanced divers. For novices, the shallow sand flats shoreward of the wall are ideal. Large mounds of coral rise off the bottom which is never deeper than 35 feet (11 m).

The second and most impressive area is between the sand flats and the drop-off. The coral mounds at the lip of the drop-off are much higher and wider than elsewhere on the island. The cuts and grooves are deep—30 to 40 feet (9-12 m)—giving you a real sense of being inside a canyon if you swim through them. The whole area is a maze of caverns, tunnels and high structures with interconnecting paths. Although a dive light is recommended to fully appreciate this jumbled warren, you cannot actually get lost as there is always a way up.

The third section is the wall itself which is vertical and impressive. The growth on this wall is not as rich in sponges and gorgonians as some of the other sites, but it is still a memorable wall dive.

This location is close to the Atlantic side of the island, so the plant life on top of the reef is slightly different. Brown and green algae cover most of this area, but blocks of pillar coral and purple sea fans will break the monotony of this carpeting.

Unfortunately, because of the often adverse conditions on this side of the island, La Crevasse is not frequently visited.

One of San Salvador's natural underwater wonders is La Crevasse where divers wind their way through canyons and tunnels.

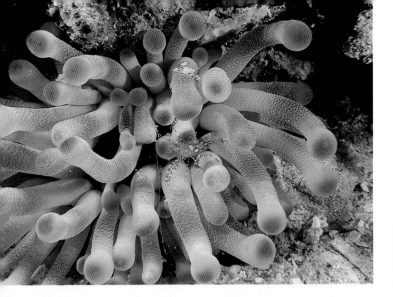

A keen eye can detect some of the underwater world's tinier creatures like this spotted cleaner shrimp in the tentacles of a giant Caribbean anemone.

The queen triggerfish, which comes in a variety of colors, is most easily identified by its electric blue markings.

CHAPTER VI SONORA BAY

Mexico

THE PAST

Sonora Bay, on the Sea of Cortez—also called the Gulf of California—in northwest Mexico, boasts a spectacular seashore with a backdrop of tawny, arid mountains.

The sea, named for the Spanish conqueror of the Aztecs, was formed several million years ago when Baja California slid abruptly west during a series of major upheavals along the San Andreas fault line.

The region of Sonora, Mexico's second largest—and second wealthiest—state, was systematically explored by the Spanish in the years after it was first reconnoitered by Coronado in 1540. The Spanish encroachment sparked the first of hundreds of years of bloody clashes with the Yaqui Indians, which continued into the early 20th century.

The area includes the old port city of Guaymas famed for its deep-sea fishing, beaches, and Mediterranean-like climate in the winter. The city, which grew up around Catholic missions dating back to 1687, is 83 miles (134 km) south of the Sonoran capital of Hermosillo, which played a key role in the fight against Spain during the Mexican Revolution of 1910.

THE PRESENT

Guaymas, now a bustling city (population 200,000) with luxury hotels and a valuable fishing industry, is in a region dominated by agriculture, particularly cotton and wheat. Mexican officials have begun planning to transform Guaymas into a "megaport" that would serve as a major trade conduit to the border city of Nogales, a principal gateway to the American southwest.

It is 20 miles (32 km) south of San Carlos Bay, a resort area that has become a model recreational community. There is a spectacular contrast in this region, where the earth tones of the desert meet the azure blue of the sea. Three miles (5 km) from San Carlos is Club Med's Sonora Bay village.

USEFUL INFORMATION

Climate. The average daily high during the winter months of December through February is about 75°F (24°C), while lows are in the mid to high 50'sF (13-15°C). April, October and November highs are usually in the low to mid-80'sF (27-30°C), and lows are in the mid-60's to low 70'sF (18-23°C). In the warmer months of May through September highs can be expected to range from 88°F (31°C) to 95°F (35°C) with nightime lows in the high 70'sF to 80°F (26-27°C). The climate is very dry except for August which may have some humidity.

Currency. The Mexican peso is the official currency, although most hotels and resorts accept travelers checks and most credit cards.

Electricity. Standard voltage is 110 volts with American sockets.

Entry and Exit Requirements. Proof of citizenship in the form of either a valid passport or birth certificate, and a return ticket are required.

Etiquette. Nude or topless bathing or sunbathing is not permitted in Mexico.

Getting There. Club Med charters fly from Phoenix, Arizona with connections to over 40 cities. The nearest airport is Guaymas about a 30-minute drive from Sonora Bay. The charters are met by buses. For those arriving independently the trip by taxi costs about US$25.

Above-water excitement abounds at Seal Island where a loud cacophony of barks greet visitors.

The Club Med Sonora Bay can also be reached by car from the United States. From Phoenix take Interstate 10 south to Tucson; from Tucson take Interstate 19 south to Nogales; from Nogales take Highway 15 south to Hermosillo and from Hermosillo take Highway 15 to Guaymas/San Carlos. At the interchange for Guaymas/San Carlos take the San Carlos exit to the right.

Language. Spanish is the national language; English, French and Spanish is spoken in the village.

Sightseeing. Club Med runs shopping trips to the local market of Guaymas and the boutiques of San Carlos.

Cruises are available to San Pedro Island—also known as Seal Island—where you can swim and snorkel near the sea lions and enjoy a picnic lunch on the boat. Also popular are sunset cruises from the San Carlos Marina featuring cocktails and music.

For fishermen, there is deep-sea fishing in the Sea of Cortez in April and May. Mountain biking, hiking in the local canyons and kayaking on the Sea of Cortez are also possibilities to explore during your stay.

In Arizona, tours can be arranged of an old Tucson film studio and the Arizona-Sonora Desert Museum. Aerial tours of the Grand Canyon or visits to the Biosphere, the sealed "ecosystem" experiment, are also available.

DINING OUTSIDE CLUB MED

La Roca   60160

Excellent Margaritas along with a variety of Mexican dishes, steak and lobster are served at this reasonably-priced restaurant in San Carlos, a 15-minute drive from the village. Tables on a terrace with an ocean view and live *mariachi* music provide a casual and local ambiance.

Papas Tapas   60707

Shrimp dishes are the specialty of Papas Tapas located on the main avenue of San Carlos. It has a large bar, reasonable prices and an extensive menu varying from local to new southwestern cuisine. Attire is casual.

El Pueblito   60777

Soft pastels and marble set the tone for this moderately- to expensively-priced restaurant

located in the new Howard Johnson Hotel, a 10-minute ride from the village. Ask about the chef's specials such as the fresh seafood combinations and the famous Sonora beef dishes. The service is excellent and a musical quartet adds to the elegant atmosphere. In addition there is live entertainment in the main bar area after dinner.

THE CLUB MED VILLAGE

The route from the airport to the village, along a flat desert road, ends with a spectacular hilltop view with the Sea of Cortez on the left, and the cactus and mountain range on the right. You almost expect cowboys to be riding alongside you at any moment. The cobblestone entrance amid 10-foot (3 m) high saguaro cactus leads to the reception plaza with its central fountain cooling the atmosphere. This area includes the offices, telephones (there are no phones in the rooms) and a well-stocked boutique.

In the same area the main restaurant serves breakfast, lunch and dinner—all buffet style. Included daily are Mexican specialties. It is air-conditioned and surrounds an enclosed patio of wild desert vegetation. Once a week there is a Mexican fiesta with the *mariachi* musicians welcoming diners at the restaurant entrance.

Two annex restaurants add diversity to your dining experience. The air-conditioned Rancho, decorated Western style, is located near the tennis courts, and is open for late breakfast and dinner. Dinner requires reservations at which time you can request a table for two (or more) where you can dine in a quiet atmosphere. The Beach restaurant, on the opposite side of the village next to the diving shack, is open for lunch and dinner, and offers a mostly seafood menu either buffet-style or served at the table.

The bar, at the center of the village, overlooks a huge swimming pool and a theater where nightly entertainment is provided. The sea center and fitness center are located in this area as well.

The muted desert colors of the Sonora Bay facility facing the Sea of Cortez are set off by lush green plants and rich blue water.

Sonora Bay provides a cool blue oasis from the arid desert climate.

A desert landscape of saguaro cactus lines the entrance of the Sonora Bay facility, welcoming its guests with a true look of the American Southwest.

KING OF THE DESERT

At the entrance to the village is a long alleyway of saguaro cactus, a prickly symbol of the American Southwest and king of the Sonoran desert. This giant cactus is known for its odd, often human-like shapes.

Summer noontime temperatures in the desert rise above 100°F (38°C) and less than 12 inches (31 cm) of rain falls here annually. The cactus is well adapted to these harsh conditions. Its accordion-like pleats allow its spongy flesh to expand and hold the water collected through its roots. The spines discourage thirsty animals and act as shade for the plant. The cactus's waxy skin further aids in reducing the loss of moisture. While the saguaro is one of the most distinctive varieties there are over fifty types of cacti living in the Sonoran desert.

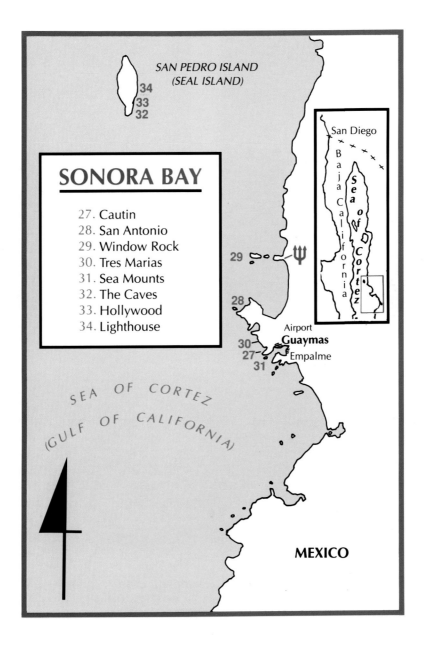

SAN PEDRO ISLAND (SEAL ISLAND)

34
33
32

SONORA BAY

27. Cautin
28. San Antonio
29. Window Rock
30. Tres Marias
31. Sea Mounts
32. The Caves
33. Hollywood
34. Lighthouse

San Diego

Baja California

Sea of Cortez

29

28

Airport
Guaymas
Empalme

30
27
31

SEA OF CORTEZ
(GULF OF CALIFORNIA)

MEXICO

The village is patterned after a Navajo Indian village, with three-story pueblo buildings that overlook the lagoon and the Sea of Cortez. The rooms are double occupancy with twin beds; some have king-size beds. Single rooms are available upon request for an extra charge. Each room has two wall safes and locks with a key. Washing machines and dryers are on both sides of the village and ice machines are located at different levels of the buildings.

The village dominates a lagoon with two large beaches, one facing south and one west. The pathway from the pool area leads to the discotheque and the water activities—water skiing, sailing, diving and wind surfing shacks.

There is a strong tennis program with 29 courts, 14 of which are lit for night play. Horseback riding (English and Western) is another highlight of Sonora Bay. A driving range for golfers is nearby, and there is a playing field which is used for baseball, football and soccer. Basketball and volleyball courts are available as well. Sonora Bay offers one of the most complete sports program of all Club Med villages.

Brilliantly colored, the colonial cup coral can usually be found in the crevices and caves of the Sea of Cortez.

A shallow reef dweller, this blenny hesitates before disappearing into its home.

Other activities are in the arts and crafts workshop where you can design your own pictures on silk, or your own jewelry. Spacious, air-conditioned conference and seminar rooms are available.

There are no special facilities for children.

DIVING—A DEDICATED DIVE CENTER

Boats. There are two main boats, the 65-foot (20 m) *Nomad* which can accommodate up to 55 divers for two-tank dives, and the *Sabrina Gale* which is 45 feet (14 m) long and can handle 32 divers on two-tank trips.

In addition, for closer sites there are two 20-foot (6 m) skiffs capable of taking 10 divers each on two-tank trips.

Certification. As a dedicated dive center both PADI and NAUI open water and advanced courses are offered. The classroom lessons are given at the sea center which is located in the village center across from the pool where most of the underwater instruction is given.

Equipment. Scubapro buoyancy compensators, Scubapro G-200 regulators with gauges and octopus rigs, and Beuchat masks and fins are standard equipment. The tanks are aluminum 80's. Wet suits and lights, if needed, are provided at no extra charge. Aladin dive computers are available for rental.

Dive Schedule. Sonora Bay is a dedicated dive center and offers two dives a day and one night dive a week. An optional third dive is available in the afternoon for which there is an extra charge. Trips are run five times a week to Seal Island, weather permitting.

Facilities. The scuba diving shack is right on the beach 150 feet (45 m) from the water. There is a large storage room where you can leave your gear for the duration of your trip, and there are hot showers and places to rinse your gear with fresh water. There is no dock so a small motor boat ferries divers from the beach to the dive boats. Although the two compressors fill the tanks at the shack, the tanks are preloaded on the dive boats by the Club Med staff.

Safety. Each dive boat is equipped with oxygen, a VHF radio and a first aid kit. Instructors and divemasters are trained in emergency first aid for scuba and other injuries. The main dive boats have two hang bars each with extra air supplied by hookah regulators. The closest recompression chamber is in San Diego and is accessible by air ambulance.

There is a doctor trained in scuba ailments located in the village, and a nurse on duty 24-hours a day.

Snorkeling. Snorkeling lessons are given at the pool after which the instructor takes the group off the beach to San Juan Island and Venado Island. Because there is boat traffic, snorkeling is best done with a guide who brings a floating dive flag.

There is no snorkeling boat for daily trips, but once a week (for an extra charge) there is a snorkeling trip to Seal Island.

In the shallow water near the village you will encounter an abundant variety of marine life including damselfishes, sergeant majors, chromis, butterflyfishes, parrotfishes and angelfishes.

Visibility. The visibility can vary between 20 and 80 feet (6-24 m). While this may seem limited compared to the Caribbean, the marine life is rich and diverse.

Water Temperature. During the winter months the water temperature can be a bit cool ranging from 65 to 70°F (18-21°C). In the summer, however the temperature is generally in the low to mid-80'sF (27-30°C).

Dive Sites

There are two distinct areas used for diving. The local sites are along the coast near the village. About a 60-minute boat ride to the north is San Pedro Island (Seal Island) where there are numerous sea lions year round. The Club Med village is in a protected nature zone and guests are requested to respect the animal and bird life and not to collect souvenirs.

Local Dives

27. CAUTIN

DEPTH:	30-80 FEET
	(9-24 M)
DISTANCE:	15 MINUTES

This site is often used as a refresher dive or for newly certified divers.

The sandy bottom gradually slopes to a maximum depth of 80 feet (24 m). Jumbles of different size rocks offer many small canyons, alcoves and caves where the marine life find protection. There are numerous angelfishes, surgeonfishes, sergeant majors, damselfishes, scorpionfish, snappers, parrotfishes and hogfish.

28. SAN ANTONIO

DEPTH:	15-50 FEET
	(5-15 M)
DISTANCE:	5 MINUTES

One of the closest dives, San Antonio is convenient for afternoon dives on one of the skiffs. Although close this site offers a large variety of marine life.

Visibility is usually good here as the site is protected by a point. In fact, when the wind is blowing south this is one of the best local spots. This area is teeming with small and juvenile fish. Among the piles of small boulders divers will find many triggerfishes who are difficult to approach closer than 3 feet (1 m). The Mexican hogfish is present here and makes a good subject for photographers. The hogfish's colors contrast nicely with the brownish environment of algae and kelp. One of the prettiest fishes you can encounter is the gray angelfish.

Swimming to the point will bring you to a very large rocky slope. Here sea horses are often seen attached to gorgonian stalks. They are only a few inches (cm) high and their camouflage is very good so you need to look very carefully to spot them.

There is usually no current to contend with so by moving slowly and observing small details, you will uncover an area teeming with small snails, sea slugs and tiny shrimps.

29. WINDOW ROCK

DEPTH:	20-80 FEET
	(6-24 M)
DISTANCE:	35 MINUTES

This is an unusual nearby dive that is located in a different bay that has little boat traffic. From the surface, Window Rock is easy to locate—it's a little rock poking out of the water with a hole in it—and is usually crawling with pelicans and other sea birds.

The underwater topography consists of a variety of peaks and large boulder formations,

An abundance of red gorgonians carpet the undersea landscape at Seal Island.

This spacious cleft in the rock is just another example of the variety of dive sites offered at Seal Island.

including the hole which divers can swim through.

The many trumpetfishes and even the large schools of jacks at this site are generally smaller than the ones further offshore. It is believed that this is an area frequented by juveniles.

Small mantas are occasionally seen here as are nurse sharks which can often be spotted lying on the sandy bottom pointing their heads under large rocks or overhangs.

30. TRES MARIAS

DEPTH:	15-45 FEET
	(5-14 M)
DISTANCE:	15 MINUTES

This site is very well protected and is commonly used for beginning divers or when the sea is rough. It is named for the three large rock towers that protrude from the water and form a point.

The lush vegetation growing on the rocks creates a green atmosphere. At 15 feet (5 m) a wall with a ledge slopes to a sandy floor at 30 feet (9 m) which continues more gradually to a sandy bottom in 45 feet (14 m) of water.

Torpedo rays, starfish, lobsters and moray eels can all be found here. Angelfishes and porcupinefish are also common. Red gorgonians add a colorful touch to this green environment.

31. SEA MOUNTS

DEPTH:	25-90 FEET
	(8-27 M)
DISTANCE:	20 MINUTES
LEVEL:	INTERMEDIATE TO
	ADVANCED

This dive, one of the best known local sites, begins at the bottom of the mooring line at a depth of 25 feet (8 m). Here there is a big jumble of rocks with steep drop-offs and some gradual descents. On top of the rock pile is a flat area which is difficult to dive because of the turbulence near the surface, and the current. The marine life, however, is very active in this zone.

One side of the rock pile descends to 75-80 feet (23-24 m), while the other drops steeply to 90 feet (27 m). Yellow hydrozone covers large areas of the rocks. Snappers and angelfishes are very common as are a variety of reef fishes such as triggerfishes, puffers, boxfish and wrasses. Because Sea Mounts is outside the bay, pelagics such as tuna, bonito and jacks are often spotted.

It is easy to get distracted by the abundance of fishes and forget to pay close attention to the marine life living on the rocks. Scorpionfish in a myriad of colors are usually found hiding on or among the rocks.

Seal Island

32. THE CAVES

DEPTH:	10-120 FEET
	(3-36 M)
DISTANCE:	60 MINUTES
LEVEL:	INTERMEDIATE TO
	ADVANCED

Located on the southern end of Seal Island is an area of huge boulders that create narrow passages and small caverns. The slope drops sharply to about 60 feet (18 m) and then levels off before continuing to depths greater than 100 feet (30 m). Big schools of fish are common here, especially in the 50- to 60-foot range (15-18 m).

The highlight of this dive is a large cavern between the wall and a huge rock slab. The entrance is about 15 feet (5 m) wide and is approximately 50 feet (15 m) high, starting 3 feet (1 m) below the surface.

Caution. When the sea is rough, surge can be strong, so stay away from the top of the cavern. Also sea lions are often cavorting inside. Be prepared to see them loom out of the interior and head for the entrance like a torpedo.

The cavern stretches for about 200 feet (61 m), and as the light diminishes considerably, a dive light will be useful. The water is generally clear as there are no particles that can be dislodged to ruin visibility. The intense blue water is a beautiful sight from the dark interior of the cavern.

There are many smaller caverns and caves located north of this main grotto. All have their entrances where the cliff levels off at around 50 to 60 feet (15-18 m).

Caution. While these caves are much smaller, some penetrate deep into the rock. Some of these are actual caves and should not be entered even with a dive light.

33. HOLLYWOOD

DEPTH:	10-65 FEET
	(3-20 M)
DISTANCE:	65 MINUTES

At the southeastern end of Seal Island not far from the caves is the Hollywood site which can be enjoyed by all levels of divers. Immediately under the boat mooring is a sandy floor which slopes gradually to about 65 feet (20 m) where the bottom is covered with an irregular landscape of boulders forming many caverns and crevices.

One huge block stands out at Hollywood. On the sea side is an overhang 30 feet (9 m) high and 15 feet (5 m) deep where a large school of grunts reside. Photographers will be pleased because these fish are not overly shy and will allow you to approach within 10 to 15 feet (3-5 m).

Female sea lions are occasionally swimming in open water, but most remain close to the wall. The unusual guitarfish can be found on the sandy bottom, but only if you have sharp eyes as they are camouflaged in the sand. A large family of colorful king angelfish are usually at the bottom of the wall swimming among the boulders. Porcupinefish, pufferfish, goatfishes and three-banded butterflyfish are all common here.

34. LIGHTHOUSE

DEPTH:	10-40 FEET
	(3-12 M)
DISTANCE:	70 MINUTES

This site, in a little bay on the leeward side of Seal Island, is especially known for its numerous sea lions. The bottom averages only 30 feet (9 m) deep and is covered with formations of round green and yellow pancake-shaped rocks. In this arena you can enjoy the show of cavorting sea lions.

Caution. You should not get too close to the pups or the bulls will charge at you with their mouths open. If this happens, back off and do not go to the surface. While no one has been injured during a confrontation, once you have been charged and seen the size of the bull's teeth, you will not want to tempt fate a second time.

On each side of the arena are big boulders which form passageways where sea lions will shoot like rockets. As the bulls keep a steady eye on divers, the females and pups will cavort around divers.

In shallow water you will also see mullet, while a little deeper are angelfishes, blue tangs and yellow goatfish.

Rarely shy in front of an audience, the sea lions at Seal Island often feature "local" underwater entertainment.

The spotted scorpionfish is a master of disguise, and divers must look closely to discern the fish from its surroundings.

CHAPTER **VII** MOOREA

French Polynesia

THE PAST

French Polynesia—the name polynesia, from the Greek words *poly* and *nesos*, means "many islands"—lies in the center of the South Pacific, halfway between Australia and the United States. The five archipelagos and 130 islands of French Polynesia are grouped into three areas: the Marquesas Islands; the Society Islands, including the Windward Islands, the most important of which are Tahiti and Moorea; and the Leeward Islands. All these islands are volcanic in origin.

The islands were gradually populated by voyagers from the Indo-Malaysian regions and the Philippines, a process that took place over several thousand years. Some archaeological excavations have traced human occupation in the Marquesas as far back as 200 B.C. Historians believe the new arrivals spread through the Pacific Ocean between 2000 and 1000 B.C. and settled in the Society Islands between A.D. 200 and 300.

Moorea once served as a refuge for warriors fleeing Tahiti and was called "Eimeo," which means "who eats hidden." It became known to Europeans as Moorea sometime between the late 18th and 19th centuries. Moorea means "yellow lizard," which was the name of the ruling Polynesian family at the time.

The island's first European visitor, in 1767, was English Captain Samuel Wallis. On April 2, 1768, French Capt. Louis Antoine de Bougainville arrived in nearby Tahiti, and upon his return to France, proclaimed the island a French possession. In 1769, another Englishman, Captain James Cook, arrived —Cook Bay on Moorea is named after him.

In 1790, Moorea was conquered by the Polynesian monarch Pomare I who was aided by 16 of the *Bounty* mutineers and their guns. He ceded Tahiti to his son Pomare II. Constant warring with other powerful factions on Tahiti forced Pomare II to flee. He regained rule of Tahiti in 1815. On June 29, 1880, Pomare V, a direct descendant, handed over the administration of Tahiti and the surrounding islands to France. In that same year the area was declared a French colony under the Third Republic.

THE PRESENT

Moorea is a 10-minute flight from Papeete, the capital of French Polynesia, which is located on Tahiti. It is smaller than Tahiti and to the northwest, separated from it by an 11-mile (18 km) channel. Moorea covers an area of 53 square miles (137 sq km), and has a coastal road that winds 37 miles (60 km) around the island.

Since 1984, French Polynesia has had self-autonomy, which allows this overseas territory to manage its own affairs while remaining part of the French Republic.

The airport, opened in 1982, is located on the northeast part of the island known as Temae Point. Tiare plantations (the tiare, of the gardenia family, is the national flower) and coconut groves stretch across this part of the coastline.

The village of Temae, surrounded by mango trees, was once the only inland village on Moorea. It is especially known for its family dance groups who used to perform for the royal court and who now entertain at the island's hotels.

The parrotfish, aptly named for its beak-like mouth, usually finds a deep crevice in which to sleep.

Moorea is a Pacific paradise, complete with lush green foliage and surrounded by turquoise lagoons and a ring of coral reefs.

Cook Bay to the northeast is protected by rugged volcanic mountains. As a result, you will feel the change in climate which goes from humid to relatively dry. The landscape, dominated by the famous Mount Rotui, includes the village of Paopao, about seven miles (11 km) from Cook Bay. The village, with its art gallery and pearl center, is a way station for boat travelers.

Opunohu Bay on the northwest coast looks a bit darker and wilder than Cook Bay and only has room for a road between the mountains and the shore.

The highest point on the island is Mount Tohive'a (3,960 feet [1,207 m]), also known as "Shark's Tooth."

A peaceful historical village set between the coastal road and a lagoon is Papetoai. Here stands an octagonal church built on the site of a former Tahitian temple that was destroyed when English Protestant missionaries made their first Christian convert. The church played an important role in the religious and political history of the island.

On the northwest point is the Tiahura district where many of the resorts, including Club Med, are located. This area gets the maximum amount of sun and the waters of the lagoon are usually perfectly smooth. The Tiki Village nearby is a reconstruction of an historical Polynesian community.

Along the east coast are the fishing villages of Haumi and Afareaitu, believed to be some of the oldest inhabited places on the island.

On either side of the road that circles the island are the villages and outlying homes of the 7,000 residents of Moorea. Many of these homes are built of bamboo and palm thatch, and are surrounded by flower gardens.

Moorea's main industries include tourism, agriculture and fishing.

USEFUL INFORMATION

Climate. The dry season runs from May through October. Frequent rains can be expected from November through April, but the length of the seasons vary slightly from year to year. Humidity is high year-round however the trade winds offer a continual respite. June through September are the coolest months with daytime highs reaching 86°F (30°) and nighttime lows falling to 68°F (20°). During the rest of the year daytime highs can reach the high 80'sF (31-32°C), while overnight lows can drop to the low 70'sF (22-23°C).

Currency. The Pacific French franc (CFP) is the official currency and is pegged to the French franc. Travelers checks and major credit cards are accepted in most establishments and at the Club Med village.

Electricity. Adapters and converters are necessary as the current is 220 volts. Dual voltage (110/220) outlets are located in the bathrooms at Club Med.

Entry and Exit Requirements. A valid passport, visa and return ticket are required. The visa is available for free at the Tahiti airport.

Etiquette. Mooreans are noted for their friendly hospitality and easygoing approach to life. Cool, comfortable clothing is recommended for sightseeing. For resort wear women may wish to try the *pareus*, a length of flowered cloth worn as a dress. Tipping is not expected.

The layout of Club Med Moorea, renovated in 1985, affords its guests privacy as well as easy access to the beach.

Getting there. Seven airlines currently offer regular service to Tahiti, which is the transfer point to Moorea. Club Med can book your flight at the time you make your village reservations. The short hop to Moorea, for which tickets must be purchased locally, takes only ten minutes. Group arrivals will be transferred by bus to the village which is about 30 minutes away. Taxis are available at the airport for those arriving independently.

Language. French and English are spoken at the village where you will also hear some of the local dialects.

Sightseeing. Tetiaroa, Marlon Brando's private atoll is a two-hour boat ride from the village. Visitors can walk from one *motu* (tiny island) to another in waist-high, crystal-clear water and also visit the pristine Bird Island.

The Club offers a bus tour of Moorea, which includes a panoramic view from Mount Belvedere overlooking both Opunohu and Cook Bay. The tour includes views of pineapple, coffee and vanilla plantations, archaeological sites, and a few stops for local shopping. Inland Moorea, with its rugged mountains, rushing streams, exotic flowers and ancient sacrificial grounds can be explored by Land Rover.

A good way to get your bearings and see the coral reef surrounding the island is to take the 20-minute helicopter ride which also overflies the mountains and two major bays.

For those who wish to go farther afield there is a trip to Bora Bora, a 50-minute flight away. There you can snorkel, take a glass bottom boat ride and watch sharks feeding.

A cruise across the channel can bring you to the local market of Papeete on Tahiti. It was on Tahiti where Paul Gauguin did many of his most famous paintings and no trip would be complete without a visit to the Gauguin Museum.

Dining Outside Club Med

Ceasarios   56-15-63

This Italian restaurant is situated on the beach right next to the Club Med village. It serves grilled steak and fish, and has a salad buffet as well as the traditional oven cooked pizza. Prices are relatively inexpensive. They are closed on Mondays.

Tiahura   56-15-45

There is a good selection of fresh seafood, prepared in either the French style or the local style at this relatively inexpensive restaurant only a two-minute walk from Club Med.

One suggestion is to try the more traditional dishes such as *poisson cru* (raw fish in lime juice). They are open daily.

Le Bateau   56-25-25

For excellent French cuisine in a romantic atmosphere try Le Bateau, a converted ferry boat now moored to a pier. There is a very good selection of dishes and wine to choose from. Besides French dishes there are a few local specialties on the menu as well. Prices are moderate and reservations are suggested. There is a free pick up service from the Club. They are open daily.

The Club Med Village

Moorea's Club Med village, built among 35 acres (14 ha) of coconut trees, was opened in 1970. The village is composed largely of bungalows—each a block of two rooms—interspersed by broad grassy areas with many beautiful flowers, including hibiscus and the distinctively perfumed tiare.

In the village center is a cocktail lounge, dance floor and theater where evening entertainment is presented. The main restaurant, across from the welcome plaza, is open air with a thatched roof. It offers breakfast, lunch and dinner buffet style at tables for eight. The food is international and includes some local specialties and a special selection of Japanese dishes. Once a week, there is a Tahitian Day with a buffet of many local specialities followed by a Tahitian show.

Facing the lagoon is Le Tiki, a thatched roof

open air restaurant, offering a sit-down dinner at tables for two or more. The specialty is seafood and a buffet of appetizers, salad and fruits. Reservations are required.

The wooden bungalows, each with a shingled roof, are comfortable, double-occupancy lodgings with private bathrooms with shower. There are ceiling fans and shutters opening to the balmy trade winds, and each room includes oversized twin beds. Extra cots are available, as well as some king-size beds. Single rooms are subject to availability at an extra charge. There are no safes in the rooms, but they do lock.

The activities include tennis with five asphalt courts—four are lit for night play—water skiing on the lagoon in front of the village, aerobics, basketball, Ping-Pong, bocci, volleyball, card and board games, and aquatic gymnastics. For an additional charge there is bicycling, horseback riding and deep-sea fishing outside the village.

Champagne sunset cruises and lobster dinner cruises are other activities available.

Cars can be rented at the Club and parking is available. Irons and ironing boards are available, but there are no laundry facilities on the Club Med grounds; they are within walking distance from the village. Ice machines are conveniently located in the village.

There are no special facilities for children, but families with children age 4 and over are welcome.

No paradise is complete without a beautiful sunset. In the evening, Moorea's sky and sea are brushed with enchanting hues.

The luxurious foliage of palm trees and island vegetation surrounding the accommodations reminds guests that they are indeed in a natural paradise.

DIVING—A DEDICATED DIVE CENTER

Boats. The main dive boat is the 40-foot (12 m) *Pareva*, an aluminum catamaran with two outboard engines that cruises at 20 knots. It is capable of carrying 40 divers for two-tank dives. The second boat is the *Pareva II*, which carries a maximum of 12 divers on one-tank dives.

Certification. As a dedicated dive center, PADI and NAUI open water and advanced certifications are available as is the Club Med resort course.

Equipment. The village is equipped with Scubapro R-190 regulators with gauges and octopus rigs, and Scubapro buoyancy compensators. Fins and masks are Beuchat, Dacor and Scubapro. The tanks are Scubapro steel 72's. Aladin dive computers and wet suits are available for rental.

Dive Schedule. There are two dives per day. There is an additional cost for the weekly night dive. This the is only Dedicated Dive Center that does not have an optional third dive of the day.

Facilities. The thatched roof dive shack where you will pick up most of your dive gear is about 100 feet (30 m) from the dock. The weights remain on the dock and the tanks stay on the boat, and are filled via a high pressure line from the two compressors. A storage room where you can leave your equipment, and fresh water rinses and showers are next to the scuba shack.

The snorkeling shack is attached to the scuba center and provides snorkeling equipment.

Safety. A Boston Whaler, which can be used for emergency evacuation, always accompanies the dive boat. Oxygen and first aid equipment are on the dive boats, and instructors and divemasters are trained to handle medical emergencies. Boats are also equipped with radios to summon assistance if needed. While there is no scuba doctor in the village, a recompression chamber is available in Papeete, a ten-minute helicopter ride away. Two decompression bars with hookah regulators for emergency air are hung 15 feet (5 m) below the dive boat.

Buddy divers who both have dive computers can dive to 130 feet (39 m), while those without computers are limited to 100 feet (30 m). All divers are restricted to no-decompression diving.

Snorkeling. A Polynesian pirogue takes snorkelers to two small islands in front of the village. The clarity of the water here is astounding. The reef in this area has sustained some damage from typhoons, but is in the process of revitalizing itself. Marine life is prolific with large schools of surgeonfishes and triggerfishes. Butterflyfishes will also be seen, and if you are lucky you might get to see whitetip or blacktip reef sharks.

Caution. Be sure to look out for poisonous stonefish and scorpionfish which could be lying camouflaged on top of the reef. Also don't get too close to the edge of the reef where breaking waves can cause a dangerous surge.

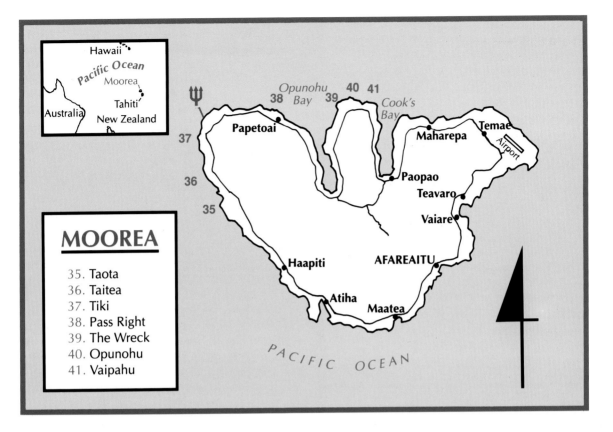

MOOREA

35. Taota
36. Taitea
37. Tiki
38. Pass Right
39. The Wreck
40. Opunohu
41. Vaipahu

The Pareva *quickly whisks divers through the lagoon on their way to another glimpse of Moorea's underwater landscape.*

Visibility. Visibility normally ranges from 100 to 200 feet (30-61 m) except in bays and channels during periods of tidal changes.

Water Temperature. There are no seasonal changes in the water temperature, but it does fluctuate between 73°F (23°C) and 82°F (28°C).

DIVE SITES

35. TAOTA

DEPTH:	3-60 FEET
	(1-18 M)
DISTANCE:	20 MINUTES

Taota Pass is on the west coast of Moorea in the Haapiti district. This site, which is a good dive for beginners when the sea is calm, includes narrow canyons that cut into the reef. Using one of these canyons, divers can actually swim all the way into the lagoon from outside the reef.

In some areas the many different size canyons form a maze, creating numerous caverns and crevices where there is an abundance of marine life, especially butterflyfishes, angelfishes, snappers and surgeonfishes.

Stay in the shallow reef area, for if you follow the gradual slope into deeper water you will come to a portion of reef mostly covered with dead coral. There is a scarcity of fishes here as well, though you may get a glimpse of a few jacks or a whitetip reef shark.

Caution. Even in a calm sea, the surge can be strong in shallow water near the reef. Also during times of strongest tidal change, be careful of areas where the canyon is shaped like a funnel which can increase the effect of the current.

36. TAITEA

DEPTH:	12-100 FEET
	(12-30 M)
DISTANCE:	20 MINUTES
LEVEL:	INTERMEDIATE

The mooring at this site is at the edge of a moderate drop-off.

The drop-off descends by steps, the platforms of which stretch about 50 feet (15 m) before dropping to the next step. The most interesting depth is in the 60-foot (18 m) range.

Multicolored clumps of coral are encountered here growing on the skeletons of the dead coral that composes most of this reef. Schools of juvenile damselfishes find refuge in the abundant acropora coral. Striped triggerfish and large yellowhead triggerfish are often seen singly as they seek out food at the top of the reef. Many butterflyfishes and redtail surgeonfish inhabit this site. The surgeonfish will attract you with the beautiful spot on each side of its tail. It is common to get a fleeting glimpse of sharks, but they are usually shy at this site.

37. TIKI

DEPTH:	40-80 FEET
	(12-24 M)
DISTANCE:	15 MINUTES

This dive spot, which faces the Club's Tiki Restaurant, is only about 200 to 300 yards (182-273 m) from the scuba dock, but it takes 15 minutes to get there because the boat has to circumvent the reef through the Taotai Pass.

As the boat approaches the permanent mooring, an incredible number of fish gather. Once you enter the water and begin your descent to the almost flat bottom at 50 feet (15 m), you will be surrounded by hundreds of bluestriped snappers, butterflyfishes, longnosed emperors, black triggerfish, and some groupers.

The density of fish life is no coincidence, for the dive leader is carrying a large fish head. On the bottom the divers have been briefed to put their backs against the reef. The fish head is attached to the bottom in the middle of the semicircle. A minute or two later, the first of the curious sharks will arrive. As more gather, they begin to make passes at the bait until one overcomes his caution and takes the first bite. At that point a feeding frenzy usually begins featuring mostly blacktip and gray sharks ranging from 3 to 6 feet (1-2 m) long. On occasion a lemon shark will appear, recognizable by its two identical dorsal fins and very small beige or yellow eyes. The lemon sharks also tend to be larger than the others, sometimes up to 9 feet (3 m).

During the feeding, a myriad of small reef fishes dart about snatching the floating scraps of food. The show lasts about ten minutes, after which the sharks realize there is nothing more to interest them and they move off into deeper water.

Another feature of this dive is a very large and friendly Napoleon fish which must weigh over 100 pounds (45 kg). It will usually appear at the beginning of the dive begging for food.

Clown fish are not affected by the anemone's sting and use this to their gastronomical advantage when less fortunate species are trapped by the anemone.

Night diving provides opportunities for close-up fish portraits like this soldierfish nestled among the coral.

Swimming among Moorea's abundant schools of sea life is just one of the pleasures of diving in the island's transparent waters.

38. THE PASS RIGHT

DEPTH:	25-80 FEET
	(8-24 M)
DISTANCE:	10 MINUTES

This is the first dive spot outside the Taotai Pass. The underwater topography is undulating in a series of valleys ranging from 30 to 60 feet (9-18 m) long that are on a gradual incline without any straight drop-offs.

Large schools of black triggerfish, yellow butterflyfish, striped butterflyfish, and grunts by the dozen will surround divers at this site. Also found here are 2-foot (62 cm) long rainbow runners which will keep circling divers until they are as close as a foot (31 cm) from your mask. They are looking for a handout as this site had been used for the shark-feeding dive before it was moved to Tiki. It is still common to see sharks—mostly whitetip and blacktip—at this location.

39. THE WRECK

DEPTH:	15-80 FEET
	(5-24 M)
DISTANCE:	15 MINUTES

This dive spot is located in the Opunohu Pass. The remains of more than one ship that wrecked trying to get into the protected Opunohu Bay lie scattered here on the ocean floor. Storms and typhoons have dismantled the wrecks, and jumbled them together so it is difficult to tell one from another.

The dive begins in 15 feet (3 m) of water where there is a large engine which serves as a magnet for marine life. Surgeonfishes, butterflyfishes, squirrelfishes and many other species find refuge within the remains. Because of the shallow depth, it is very bright

A side trip of interest is to Moorea's neighboring island of Tetiaroa, which is home to many frigate birds such as this young one.

and you can peer inside the engine without needing a dive light. Photographers can shoot here with available light.

Follow the crack down the wall of the coral reef until you reach a depth of 60 feet (18 m). At this point, turn right and swim for about 100 yards (91 m) where you will come to more pieces of scattered wreckage including the skeleton of a hull.

Depending on the current and the tide, the water can either be very clear or murky. The wreckage is the main attraction of this site since the fish live on the deeper portions of the reef. That doesn't mean you won't be lucky since octopus are occasionally spotted here.

40. OPUNOHU

DEPTH:	30-100+ FEET
	(9-30+ M)
DISTANCE:	20 MINUTES

Opunohu, which means "mouth of the stonefish," is located beyond the Wreck site. It is still very close to the channel of Opunohu and visibility can be strongly affected by the outgoing tide from the Bay.

Beginners may prefer to stay on top of the drop-off which is about 30 to 40 feet (9-12 m) deep, while intermediate and advanced divers may wish to proceed down the drop-off which bottoms out at approximately 100 feet (30 m). The wall is fairly steep but is not vertical.

Marine life is abundant all along the reef and drop-off, but there are three points of interest.

First, there is a very large moray eel whose hole is in the 50 to 60 foot (15-18 m) range. It is used to being fed, and will come out of its hole and approach divers which can be a frightening experience for novices. Do not point your hands in the moray's direction (especially if you are wearing shiny jewelry) because he could mistake your fingers for a handout. Moray eels are not ferocious, but they appear so because their mouths must be open to draw water over their gills. It is strongly recommended never to feed these animals. Even if you are not harmed, the next diver might not be so lucky.

The second point of interest is a large old anchor resting in 60 feet (18 m) of water. To get to this anchor you need to swim at least 200 or 300 yards (182-273 m) from the mooring in the direction of the pass. This is a long swim so be sure to monitor your air supply. The anchor makes a great backdrop for photographers.

The third point of interest is a very large anemone hosting clownfish which can be found halfway between the mooring and the anchor in about 45 feet (14 m) of water.

41. VAIPAHU

DEPTH:	40-130+ FEET
	(12-39 M)
DISTANCE:	25 MINUTES
LEVEL:	INTERMEDIATE TO
	ADVANCED

There are two specific sections to this site. First, follow the canyon to a depth of 110 feet (33 m) where you will discover *montipora* coral in the shape of huge roses reaching 9 to 12 feet (3-4 m) in diameter. These formations stretch along the reef for as far as the eye can see in the very clear water and can be found to a depth of 160 feet (48 m). At this point the wall drops vertically into the abyss. Fortunately a depth of 130 feet (39 m) is ideal for a panoramic view of the coral field. Blacktip, nurse and occasional lemon sharks are usually spotted here.

The second section of this site is made up of a succession of coral ridges at a depth of around 60 feet (18 m). Grunts, black triggerfish, striped triggerfish and giant yellowhead triggerfish are prolific along the reef. Many butterflyfishes add a colorful touch to the reef. Crevices and caverns offer sanctuary for squirrelfishes and moray eels.

CHAPTER VIII BUCCANEER'S CREEK

Martinique

THE PAST

Martinique, in the heart of the Lesser Antilles, was known to the Carib Indians as *Madinina*, or the island of flowers. Its brilliant, lushly vegetated hillsides so entranced Columbus—who is believed to have visited the island on his fourth voyage in 1502—that he declared it the most fertile, charming, and beautiful place he had ever seen.

This mountainous island, of volcanic origin—one volcano, Mt. Pelée, remains active—was settled about A.D. 100 by the Arawak Indians who had emigrated to the region from South America. Their peaceful, agricultural society ultimately fell under repeated attacks by the predatory Caribs.

After the Spanish conquistadores had carried their relentless search for gold to richer pastures, a Norman nobleman named Pierre Belain d'Esnambuc arrived with a group of French colonists and built Fort St. Pierre, from which they fought a running war against the Caribs. Within 25 years, the Indians had been all but exterminated, the survivors fleeing to St. Vincent and Dominica. The French proceeded to expand their sugar plantations, importing African slaves to work the fields. By 1640, sugar was a booming industry on Martinique.

As was the case with other islands in the region, Martinique was the scene of see-saw occupations by England and France in the 17th and 18th centuries. The British seized the island in 1762, returning it soon as part of a swap with France for Canada, Senegal, and the islands of Tobago, St. Vincent, and the Grenadines.

Martinique was the birthplace on June 23, 1763 of Marie-Josephe Rose Tascher de La Pagerie, the future Empress Josephine of France. At the age of 16, she was married to the son of a former governor of Iles du Vent. The couple eventually separated and her husband was sent to the guillotine during the Revolution. Six years later Josephine married a then unknown general. His name was Napoleon Bonaparte. She was never again to return to Martinique.

Martinique was reoccupied by the British from 1794 to 1802 at the request of plantation owners alarmed by Revolution-inspired slave uprisings on Guadeloupe and other French Caribbean colonies. After France reclaimed the island, it took nearly half a century before slavery was finally abolished in 1848, the result of years of struggle led by Victor Schoeler, Martinique's greatest hero.

Disaster struck Martinique suddenly when Mt. Pelée erupted on May 8, 1902, devastating the entire city of St. Pierre, killing more than 30,000 people. There was only one known survivor in the village, a drunk who had been jailed for the night.

Martinique was declared a French department in 1946, and a region in 1974. Its citizens are French; its administrative and political structures are identical to those of France.

THE PRESENT

Martinique's administrative body, the Prefecture, sits in Fort de France, which is also the island's commercial and cultural capital.

Geologically, the northern two-thirds of the island are dominated by dramatic volcanic peaks and steep coasts, with the south characterized by vast white sand beaches.

A stroll through the winding paths of Buccaneer's Creek village is scented by the sweet fragrance of bougainvillea.

The natural beauty of the island, along with its inland hamlets and traditional fishing villages, have combined to make tourism a major factor in Martinique's economic growth. Its other principal sources of income are sugar, rum, pineapples, bananas, juices and other fruit-derived products.

USEFUL INFORMATION

Climate. The temperature averages about 79°F (26°C), but at the highest elevations it can be as cool as 63°F (17°C). Daytime highs can reach the high 80'sF (30-32°C) with evenings usually in the mid-70'sF (24°C). The summer months are several degrees warmer than the winter months. The east and northeast trade winds make even the hottest days comfortable. From the end of August through October you can expect to have occasional rain showers.

Currency. The French franc is the legal tender. Most establishments accept credit cards, travelers checks and U.S. dollars.

Electricity. Outlets are 220 volts, 50 cycles, making adapters and converters a necessity for many visitors. However, 110/220 outlets are available in the bathrooms at the Club Med village.

Entry and Exit Requirements. No vaccinations are required for French, American or Canadian citizens, but passports and return tickets are.

Etiquette. Dress in Martinique tends to be light and informal—swimsuits, sandals and shorts. Evenings call for light resort wear, but jackets are required at many top restaurants and casinos. Martinique is distinctive for its friendly hospitality. Topless sunbathing is acceptable.

Getting There. Air France and several American airlines fly to Martinique. Club Med provides weekly charter service from New York and Miami, as well as transfers from the airport to Buccaneer's Creek. The Club Med village is about a 45-minute drive from the airport; the taxi fare is about 350 francs. Rental cars are available at the airport, with parking at the village.

Language. The official language is French although English is also spoken at the Club Med village. You will also hear a Creole patois which consists of words borrowed from Spanish, English and French, and is influenced by some African languages.

Sightseeing. Club Med offers sunset cruises and lobster dinners aboard *La Nuit Des Temps*, a 51-foot (15 m) sailing ketch. Also available are deep-sea fishing, shopping tours, casino excursions and visits to points of interest such as Les Gorges de la Falaise. This magnificent stretch of rain forest along the Atlantic coast, within sight of Mt. Pelée, boasts a spectacular waterfall. Another spot worth visiting is Jardin de Balata, a botanical garden with more than a thousand varieties of plants. Martinique produces a distinctively flavored variety of rum, and enthusiasts can choose among nine distilleries that offer public tours.

St. Pierre, completely rebuilt since its destruction in the 1902 eruption of Mt. Pelée, has a museum of artifacts and displays from the disaster, including the jail cell where the lone survivor was held.

Those interested in exploring neighboring islands can arrange for daylong excursions to such places as Dominica and the Grenadines, which are readily accessible by plane and catamaran.

July in Fort de France is festival time, a cavalcade of plays, ballets and other performances by local and foreign artists.

The island is home to a folk ballet company, a 30-member group that has represented Martinique in performances worldwide.

During the first two weeks of December, many world-renowned musicians appear at the jazz or guitar festival. Jazz is featured in odd-numbered years with guitar in even years.

As elsewhere in the French West Indies, Carnival begins several weeks before Ash Wednesday with parades and street dances every weekend, climaxing with an exotic finale on Ash Wednesday.

DINING OUTSIDE CLUB MED

Poï et Virginie   76-72-22

Located on the water in the little village of St. Anne, about a 20-minute walk along the beach from Club Med is this moderately-priced restaurant with a local atmosphere. Caribbean specialties such as grilled fish, lobster and various salads are served.

Secluded on a protected bay, Buccaneer's Creek provides a respite from the hustle and bustle of the more touristed areas of Martinique.

Sunny   76-76-74

Lobster and stuffed crab are the specialties at Sunny, which has a very relaxed atmosphere and is only a five-minute walk down the beach from the Club Med village.

Le Point de Vue   74-74-40

Aptly named for its magnificent panoramic hilltop view, this restaurant specializes in Creole and French dishes. It is about a 20-minute drive from Club Med, past the city of Marin, on the other side of the bay. Terrace dining with a view of Club Med is available. Prices are moderate to expensive. This is also a great place to enjoy a cocktail.

THE CLUB MED VILLAGE

The Creole-inspired Club Med village of Buccaneer's Creek is on the island's extreme south coast near the city of St. Anne. Completed in 1969, its secluded beach faces the landmark Rocher du Diamant (Diamond Rock), a huge volcanic boulder that was once occupied by British cannoneers in the 18th century.

The 48-acre (19 ha) village, visible to approaching guests through a grove of coconut palms, features a main street that winds past the lodgings in a setting of lush tropical foliage of bougainvillea, papaya, fire trees and other distinctively Caribbean flora.

The village is dominated by a domed complex overlooking the sea that includes a dance floor, theater, dining room and bar.

The beach, which stretches for miles, includes separate areas close by for water skiing, and shacks near the marina for snorkeling, scuba diving and wind surfing. The immediate area is dotted with palm trees and dominated by the Tour de Port, a conical building overlooking the water that is the resort's most distinctive feature. Sun-splashed and busy by day, it is romantic and magical by night.

The Tour du Port at sunset represents the flavor of Buccaneer's Creek.

The surrounding area includes seven composition-surface tennis courts, six of which are equipped for night play.

At the end of the village where the beach curves away from the lodgings is a popular, open-air discotheque. A thatched-roof structure houses the Yacht Club, an annex restaurant that serves buffet-style meals featuring fish and other local fare. It is convenient for those already on the beach who don't want to walk back to the main restaurant at the village center. Reservations, however, are necessary.

The Tour du Port includes a bar and an area that serves breakfast for late risers.

The main restaurant, its ambiance enhanced by the sounds of songbirds in the nearby gardens, offers seating at tables for eight on two floors, both of which overlook the water. It features hot and cold buffets representing both local and international tastes.

Rooms are air-conditioned, double and triple occupancy, and situated in two- and three-story beach- and garden-front lodgings. Each room has high, twin four-poster beds; some rooms have queen-size beds.

Single rooms, which require an extra charge, are subject to availability. Rooms include safes and individual keys; ice machines are nearby.

Besides water skiing, snorkeling, wind surfing and scuba diving, Buccaneer's Creek offers volleyball, basketball, bocci, Ping-Pong, soccer, aerobics, calisthenics and even picnicking. For an extra fee you can parasail or use paddle boats and jet skis, all a short

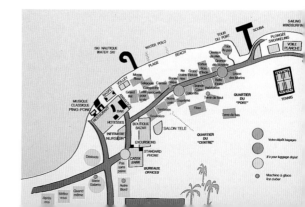

distance from the village.

Golfers can avail themselves of the Empress Josephine Golf Club in the city of Antoise, about 14 miles (23 km) from the village.

Although there are no special facilities for children, and the village is not specifically recommended for them, those over 12 are accepted.

DIVING—STANDARD PROGRAM

Boats. The village has three boats. The main dive boat is the 57-foot (17 m) *Surveyor* which cruises at 12 knots and can accommodate approximately 40 divers on one-tank trips.

The *Sandy Seas* is a cabin cruiser available for excursions on Tuesdays and Thursdays to a lovely site known as Les Anses d'Arlet for both divers (it's a two-tank trip) and snorkelers.

The *Dara* is a 36-foot (11 m) aluminum catamaran used for snorkeling.

Certification. Only Club Med certification is offered in this village; the course is given in afternoons and lasts for four days.

Dive schedule. For openwater dives there is a choice of either the 8 A.M. or 10 A.M. dive, but you are not permitted to do two dives. If you choose the early dive, on your return you can have a late breakfast on the terrace of the Tour de Port next door to the dive center.

Dive sites are mostly within a 30-minute boat ride except for the once-a-week trip to Diamond Rock. Because of local regulations, there is no openwater diving on Sunday, but the dive school is open every day of the week.

Once a week there is a night dive for divers who have logged in at least 10 previous dives.

Equipment. The village is equipped with

Scubapro 72 cubic-foot steel tanks, Scubapro R-190 regulators with gauges (metric or U.S.) and octopus regulators, Scubapro buoyancy compensators, Scubapro masks and Beuchat fins. Dive lights are also available. Wet suits are available for rental. Tanks remain on board the dive boat.

Facilities. The diving shack is less than 30 feet (9 m) from the dock, with a separate building for the compressor room which houses two Luchard Compair compressors. Tanks are filled on board the dive boat via high pressure lines running from the compressor to the dock.

Fresh water is available at the dock for rinsing tanks and dive gear. Near the scuba shack is a thatch roof shelter used for instructions, sign-ups and meetings. There are no lockers or storage facilities available, but the village provides bags for carrying dive gear.

Safety. A doctor trained in scuba medicine and a divemaster are always on board the dive boat. Oxygen and medical kits are on board, as well as a VHF radio to reach Samu, the French Government rescue agency. Samu operates a recompression chamber in Fort de France and can arrange helicopter evacuation from the landing pad next to the Club Med village's disco. A 17-foot (5 m) Boston Whaler always accompanies the dive boat for use in emergency evacuations. There are also two nurses stationed in the village.

The main dive boat is equipped with two decompression bars at 15 feet (5 m), one on each side of the boat. These have hookah regulators for an extra air supply.

Snorkeling. The aluminum catamaran *Dara* makes morning and afternoon trips to local

A local fishing boat on the beach provides a colorful contrast to the newer sail boats in the marina.

spots. These sites are about a 10- to 20-minute trip from the village. Depth ranges between 10 and 15 feet (3-5 m), and you can expect to see reef fishes such as parrotfishes, Spanish hogfish, sergeant majors, angelfishes and butterflyfishes. A variety of colorful sponges and corals can also be seen.

Snorkeling equipment is provided and must be returned at the end of each snorkeling outing. The bay in front of the village can become crowded with powerboats and wind surfers, so it is suggested that even if you have your own equipment you limit your snorkeling to the snorkeling excursions.

Visibility. Visibility averages between 50 and 120 feet (15-36 m) depending on sea conditions.

Water temperature. During the summer season the water temperature averages about 82°F (28°C) dropping during the winter months to about 76°F (24°C).

DIVE SITES

42. SMALL WALL

DEPTH:	15-50 FEET
	(5-15 M)
DISTANCE:	10 MINUTES

Below the boat mooring in about 15 feet (5 m) of water is the top of the reef on which sea fans, barrel sponges, leaf and saucer corals have attached themselves to a mass of dead coral.

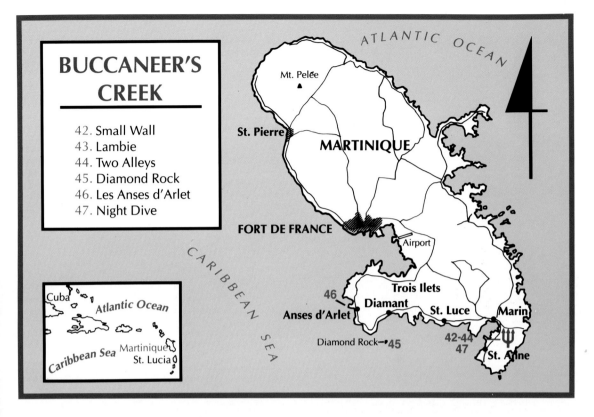

BUCCANEER'S CREEK

But the highlight of this site is the 600-foot (182 m) long wall that plunges to about 50 feet (15 m). Swimming to the right (facing seaward) will take you to a large rock where there are numerous lobsters. Spider crabs and porcupinefish are usually abundant in this area. Although more commonly seen at night, on a lucky day you may encounter a school of squid. There is a greenish atmosphere to this site from the presence of algae.

43. LAMBIE

DEPTH:	45-130 FEET
	(14-39 M)
DISTANCE:	15 MINUTES

This site is named for the lambie, a species of conch known locally as "five fingers" which was once common here. The gentle slope is covered with sheet, star and brain corals as well as some purple leaf coral. Sea rods and sea fans cover the reef top to the edge of the descent. Crinoids, arrow crabs, parrotfishes and blue chromis are numerous. Other common

residents are triggerfishes which can be seen swimming in their clumsy style looking for small shells. Sometimes you may also encounter a school of small barracuda at the 90-foot (27 m) level.

There is little to be gained by dropping below 100 feet (30 m) as most of the interesting sights are in shallower water.

44. TWO ALLEYS

DEPTH:	50-120 FEET
	(15-36 M)
DISTANCE:	15 MINUTES

The reef, which is encircled by two 150-foot (45 m) sand alleys, begins at 50 feet (15 m). By swimming over the reef toward deeper water, you will come to a slope that descends gradually to 120 feet (36 m).

This site is not teeming with reef fishes, but there are many little holes and crevices in the reef which make ideal sanctuaries for small fish and invertebrates. If you take the time to look carefully in these holes, you will see

Diamond Rock was once garrisoned by the British until retaken by the French in 1805. It is now a haven for thousands of birds.

many species of marine life including squirrelfishes and arrowcrabs. Spidercrabs and lobsters can also be seen hiding in deep recesses.

Keep glancing towards the deeper water, for on a good day you might see tarpon or jacks cruising by.

45. DIAMOND ROCK

DEPTH:	50-100 FEET (15-30 M)
DISTANCE:	60 MINUTES
LEVEL:	INTERMEDIATE TO ADVANCED

This volcanic rock, rising up out of the sea off the southern coast, is a refuge for thousands of birds. In the early 1800's it was garrisoned by

the British navy until retaken by the French in 1805.

The dive boat moors on the protected side of the rock in 100 feet (30 m) of water. The intense blue water is usually very clear with over 100-foot (30 m) visibility. It is important not to drop too deep initially in order to save bottom time for sights closer to the rock. The main point of interest is not the marine life, but the jumbles of large boulders which create small caves and overhangs carpeted with colorful gorgonians and sponges.

Beyond the boulders is a cave which is about

A dive at Diamond Rock is not complete without a swim through the cave that cuts across the south point.

Schools of blackbar soldierfish can usually be found hiding in dark recesses at depths between 15 and 60 feet (5-18 m).

With its pouty mouth and honeycombed markings, the honeycomb cowfish is easily identified and can be approached quite closely at night.

50 feet (15 m) beneath the surface. It is approximately 15 feet (5 m) wide and 50 feet (15 m) high, and if the sea is rough you can clearly hear the waves smashing against the grotto above. Avoid getting too close to the turbulence at the surface. The entrance to the cave is very colorful with a large school of squirrelfishes usually on view.

Caution. The cave is about 200 feet (61 m) long, and while it is always clear, traversing its entire length involves crossing under a portion of the rock and exiting in another location. From any point inside the cave you can see the blue water of both entrances, but with all overhead environments special caution should be observed.

After passing through the cave, keep the cliff on your left and you will come to a cavern in the 40- to 50-foot (12-15 m) depth range. Continuing on will bring you to another cut in the wall, this one about 150 feet (45 m) wide and in 30 feet (9 m) of water.

Caution. It is important to keep track of your bearings and your air supply to be able to easily return to the boat. In addition, the current can be strong depending on the tide and wind conditions.

46. LES ANSES D'ARLET

DEPTH:	30-80 FEET
	(9-24 M)
DISTANCE:	75 MINUTES

There is a fee charged for this excursion which is open to both scuba divers and snorkelers. Included are two dives and lunch in a local restaurant on the beach in Les Anses d'Arlet. The trip to this bay on the other side of the island is made on the comfortable cabin cruiser *Sandy Seas*.

Visibility is spectacular, often reaching over 150 feet (45 m), and marine life is more abundant than on the Club Med side of the island. The morning dive usually takes place on the southern point of Les Anses d'Arlet where the depth reaches 60 feet (18 m). Piles of rocks create many hidden places for squirrelfishes. There is a rock split by a large fissure where a school of about 50 squirrelfishes gather. Many colorful sponges

and concretions attached to the rock make this an ideal photographic area. Trumpetfishes are surprisingly common here and jacks are often seen towards the open water.

The afternoon dive is on the other side of the bay where there is another jumble of boulders and colorful tube sponges. Although the site bottoms out at about 80 feet (24 m) the best scenery is in the 40- to 60-foot (12-18 m) range.

Unfortunately for the environment, there are many abandoned fish traps in the area still catching fish. Local fishermen who lose their bamboo and iron traps tend to build new ones instead of retrieving those they have lost.

47. NIGHT DIVE

DEPTH:	15-50 FEET
	(5-15 M)
DISTANCE:	10 MINUTES

Night dives are organized at Green Buoy, Red Buoy or Little Wall. These three dive locations offer excellent topography for divers of all levels.

Night is a special time on the reef when those fishes and invertebrates which hide during the day come out to hunt and forage. Crabs, lobsters and shrimp can be observed closely. For some, there is the temptation to try to grab a lobster. Not only is it prohibited, but the spiny lobster has a defense. If grabbed by the antenna, it will break free with a powerful kick of its tail, leaving its antenna in your hand. Lobsters injured in this way become easy prey for the octopus population.

Basket starfish open at night and can often be seen adorning sea fans while spreading their arms to feed on passing plankton. Moray eels come out of their holes and swim in the open water searching for food. Night diving provides many opportunites for photographers.

CHAPTER **IX**   CANCUN

Mexico

THE PAST

The resort city of Cancun is on a 14-mile (23 km) long sandbar a quarter of a mile (.16 km) wide at the northeastern tip of Mexico's Yucatan Peninsula. It is separated from the mainland by two small canals on either end which unite the Nichupte Lagoon with the turquoise waters of the Caribbean.

The name "Cancun" comes from the Mayan civilization, one of the world's greatest Indian cultures, and means "Pot of Snakes". During the Mayan period, which began about A.D. 600 the area was populated by an industrious and cultured race. The Mayans who settled here in vast autonomous city-states grew vegetables, fruits, and medicinal plants. Today the archaeological ruins of their cities lie scattered in the jungle attracting an increasing number of tourists. While chicle and sisal were the principal agricultural products for centuries, tourism has now become the backbone of the economy.

THE PRESENT

Cancun, one of the leading tourist destinations in Mexico, didn't exist in its current form before 1974, when the Mexican Government decided to build a resort that would provide employment for those living on the Yucatan, and give a boost to the national economy. Cancun was selected because it offers the best of the Caribbean with almost constant sun. Between its beaches, its new hotels and the proximity of the Mayan ruins this former fishing village of coconut plantations and chicle trees has become an internationally known resort.

Cancun is divided into two areas. There is the luxurious hotel zone with the Caribbean on one side and the lagoon on the other, and there is Cancun City which houses the workers who make their living from the hotel zone. Cancun City is known for its shopping. There one can find everything from designer labels to traditional Mexican arts and crafts.

USEFUL INFORMATION

Climate. The average daily temperature is 80°F (27°C). Winter highs reach the mid-80's F (29-30°C), while overnight lows rarely drop below 70°F (21°C). Daytime highs during the summer months reach 90°F (32°C) with lows of about 75°F (24°C). There are approximately 240 days of sunshine a year.

Currency. The Mexican Peso is the standard currency although travelers checks and most major credit cards are accepted in most stores and restaurants.

Electricity. The current in the Club Med village is 110 volts with standard American sockets.

Entry and Exit Requirements. Valid passports are required. Children traveling with one parent must have a notarized statement from the other parent authorizing travel outside the United States. There is a departure tax of U.S.$11.50.

Etiquette. Nude or topless bathing or sunbathing is not permitted in Mexico.

Getting There. Club Med does not run its own charter flights to Cancun. However, Mexican and American carriers offer regular flights. Cancun Airport is about 6 miles (10 km) from the Club Med village, which is about a 20-minute taxi ride.

Surrounded by a reef, this protected reserve in Cancun makes a perfect place to snorkel.

Language. Spanish is the national language. English, French and Spanish are spoken in the village.

Sightseeing. No visit to Cancun would be complete without a trip to the excavated Mayan ruins. Chichen-Itza, a half-day excursion by plane or a full day by bus, is the largest and best restored of the Mayan sites. The pyramid and observatory are monuments of ancient astronomical knowledge. This site was the ceremonial and administrative center of the Mayan civilization during its so-called classical period from A.D. 900 to 1200. The ruins exhibit the influence of the Maya, and the Toltec, a warrior tribe that conquered many of the Mayan city-states.

Another half-day tour is to Tulum, a Mayan fortress overlooking the sea, that has the only surviving frescoes in the Yucatan Peninsula. You can snorkel in the lagoon of Xel-ha below the fortress.

The most recently found inland site of Coba was never discovered by the Spanish. It juts out of the jungle, still partially overgrown by vegetation.

A 45-minute boat ride to the north of Cancun is Isla Mujeres, a small island with a very relaxed local atmosphere. This secluded island boasts long stretches of beaches and excellent snorkeling reefs.

Other excursions outside the village are deep sea fishing, horseback riding, shopping trips and even bullfights.

Time. Cancun is in the Central Standard Time Zone and does not observe Daylight Savings Time.

DINING OUTSIDE OF CLUB MED

There are hundreds of restaurants of every variety and price range in Cancun. The following are just three suggestions:

Lorenzillos   3-1254

Lorenzillos is a moderately- to expensively-priced restaurant that has a warm nautical atmosphere and overlooks the water in the hotel zone. Two of the specialties of this popular seafood dining spot are lobster and soft shell crab. Reservations are advised.

El Mexicano   3-2220

For excellent Mexican dishes, including a variety of regional dishes from all over the country, try El Mexicano located in the La Mansion-Costa Blanca Shopping Center, in the hotel zone after the point of Cancun. Live *mariachi* music, a folkloric show and an elegant colonial setting create a special atmosphere. Prices are moderate to expensive and reservations are advised.

Bogart's   3-1133

Located in the Krystal Cancun Hotel by the point of Cancun is Bogart's, an elegant and exclusive restaurant. The decor, with arches and palm trees, is reminiscent of Humphrey Bogart's movie "Casablanca" set in North Africa. A pianist playing a large white piano in the middle of the main room adds to the atmosphere. The food is excellent and includes many international dishes including Arabic specialties. Reservations are advised for this expensive restaurant.

THE CLUB MED VILLAGE

The Club Med village was built in 1976 and renovated in 1989. It sits on 38 acres (15 ha) and can accommodate up to 820 guests. It is situated on the far eastern tip of Cancun at Punta Nizuc (Windy Point).

The village, which resembles an ancient Mayan city, is long and narrow. From the gate it's quite a ride to reach the welcome plaza in the center of the village. The pyramid-shaped main building is built around a huge atrium. The bar, dance floor, theater and main restaurant, decorated with Mexican ceramics and tapestries are all located here. A large oval swimming pool with a pool-side bar and lounge opens onto the beach. The offices and telephones (there are no phones in the rooms) are to the right of the pool facing the beach.

Because the village is on a point there are long stretches of beach on two sides. In the middle is the lagoon which comes right up to the buildings.

The main restaurant is near the pool and serves buffet meals. The El Rancho annex turns into the disco at night and is located by the water on the point. Further down the beach towards the water sports area is La Palapa, a

Early morning visitors can relax in solitude next to the large swimming pool located at the center of the village.

thatched roof restaurant built on pilings over the water. Both annexes serve buffet lunch and offer a romantic setting for dinner. In both these restaurants you can request a table for two (or more), and reservations are necessary for dinner. Once a week is Mexican night with Mexican specialties, *mariachi* music, and a performance by the Ballet Folklorico of Cancun.

The accommodations consist of two- and three-story buildings with many terraces, facing either the lagoon or the sea. The air-conditioned rooms are double occupancy with

Club Med Cancun is situated directly on a lagoon which provides an unusual setting for guests.

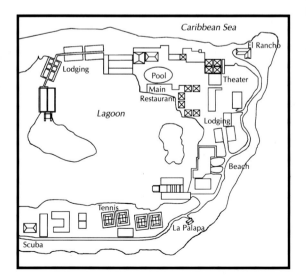

twin beds and are decorated with a Mexican motif. All have safes and keys. Single rooms are available on request for an extra charge.

You can either take the shuttle bus or walk along the beach road to the scuba shack and the facilities for wind surfing and sailing. Water skiing is done in both the ocean and the lagoon. There are eight composition tennis courts, four of which are lit for night play. For an extra charge you can parasail at the beach. An 18-hole golf course is approximately eight miles (13 km) from the Club.

Near the boutique and facing the lagoon is the fitness center. The sea center, where divers view special presentations and sign up for dives, is located under the main restaurant.

Laundry facilities with irons and ironing boards are available. Ice machines are conveniently located. Cars can be rented at the airport or in town and there is parking at the Club.

There are no special facilities for children so this village is recommended for ages 12 and over.

DIVING—STANDARD PROGRAM

Boats. The Club has one boat, the *Scuba V*, a 42-foot (13 m) V-hull with capacity for up to 35 divers for a one-tank dive.

Certification. Only the Club Med resort course is given at this village. It consists of four afternoon lessons.

Equipment. Scubapro R-190 regulators with gauges and octopus rigs, and Scubapro buoyancy compensators are standard equipment. Tanks are aluminum 80's. Beuchat fins and masks are supplied as are halogen lights for night dives. All equipment must be returned after each dive. If you need gear to go snorkeling on your own, the snorkeling shack on the other side of the village will provide it. Wet suit rentals are available in Cancun.

Dive Schedule. There is a morning dive at 8:15 and 10:15. You have a choice of times, but may sign up for only one. Because of the proximity of the dive sites the same boat makes both trips. Once a week there is a night dive. To qualify you must have at least 10 logged dives.

For divers in search of additional diving, there is a two-dive excursion to Cozumel. The cost of about U.S.$200 includes airfare (with a low-altitude return), taxis, boat and lunch. The

"Albert," along with some of his cronies, are permanent residents of the lagoon.

Tropical flowers, like this variation of the common hibiscus, decorate the village landscape.

morning dive is usually at Columbia or Palancar Reef and the afternoon dive is often at Santa Rosa Reef. These are drift dives as the current can often be very strong. Visibility almost always exceeds 100 feet (30 m). Cozumel is known for magnificent walls, and huge coral buttresses interlaced with caves and tunnels. You must have at least five logged dives to go on this trip.

Certified divers may dive as buddy teams; all others are led by an instructor.

Facilities. The thatched roof scuba shack is located near the entrance to the village which is quite a distance from the village center. Fortunately there is a shuttle going from the center to the front gate every 10 minutes.

There is a storage room at the scuba shack where you can leave your personal dive gear. Outside the storage room is a large fresh water rinse tank and showers. The two Mako compressors fill the tanks via a high pressure line to the end of the dock. Tanks remain on board at all times.

Adjacent to the shack is another thatched roof where lessons are held in the open air, and refreshments of fruit, cheese, ham and bread are served after dives.

Safety. A Boston Whaler accompanies the dive boat in case an emergency evacuation is needed. Oxygen and first aid kits are on the dive boat, and instructors and divemasters are trained in its use. There is no scuba doctor in residence at the village, but there are numerous local doctors available. There are recompression chambers in Cancun and on the nearby resort island of Cozumel.

The dive boat is equipped with two hang bars with hookah regulators for emergency air.

Snorkeling. Directly in front of the new building "Opera" is a protected reserve which forms a natural pool of water enclosed by the reef. This area is about 200 yards (182 m) wide and 500 yards (455 m) long. Access is right off the beach opposite the snorkeling shack which provides the equipment.

As you step into the water you will be welcomed by hundreds of young grunts and snappers looking for a handout. As the depth increases to the 10- to 15-foot (3-5 m) range you will see many parrotfishes, schools of jacks and an occasional barracuda that remains stationary in the water column. As menacing as it may seem to have a three-foot (1 m) barracuda watching your every move, there is little danger. If you try to swim closer he will always keep a safe distance away.

The bottom is only 15 feet (5 m) deep, but there are many varieties of coral, especially smooth and grooved brain coral, blocks of star coral, and elkhorn coral. Many small passages and canyons give the reserve a maze-like appearance. In most places you can stand and pop your head out of the water to check your bearings.

For experienced snorkelers (only when the sea is calm), there are some interesting passages cutting through the edge of the reef into the open ocean.

Schools of porkfishes are frequently seen while diving in the Mexican Caribbean. Relatively unafraid, they can usually be approached by divers.

Visibility. Visibility is variable, but usually ranges between 50 and 100 feet (15-30 m).

Water Temperature. The water temperature is fairly constant throughout the year and is generally in the mid to high 70'sF (23-26°C), reaching as high as 80°F (27°C).

DIVE SITES

48. LAS ISLAS

DEPTH:	45-60 FEET
	(14-18 M)
DISTANCE:	10 MINUTES

The mooring for this site is just outside of the channel in front of the dive shack. This is a good dive for beginners because there is no current and the depth is limited to 60 feet (18 m).

The reef consists mainly of mountainous star, smooth star, and brain coral. Covering the top of the reef are numerous sea rods and sea fans. A series of tunnels, cuts and caverns adds diversity to the topography.

It is, however, the large quantity of yellowtails and schools of grunts that have made this site popular. You will also encounter many Bermuda chub which have the ability to adjust to a variety of backgrounds by changing from light to dark or by taking on a spotted pattern. Several large whitespotted filefish are usually hanging around the mooring chain. They make great subjects for photographers and can be approached as close as 2 or 3 feet (1 m).

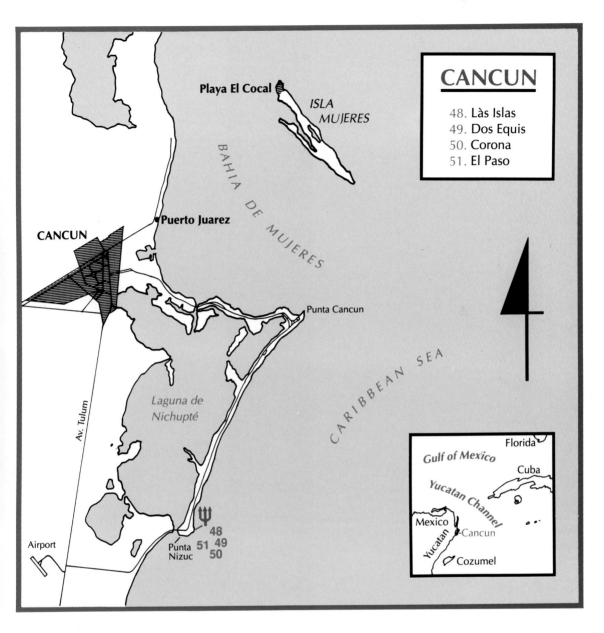

49. DOS EQUIS

DEPTH:	50-60 FEET
	(15-18 M)
DISTANCE:	15 MINUTES

Dos Equis—Spanish for "double X"—is a famous brand name of beer in Mexico, so why this dive spot got the name is a mystery. Located just a few minutes away from Las Islas, the topography is quite similar except for the two tunnels near the mooring. They are both about 100 feet (30 m) long, and lead to a section of reef that looks very much like a coffee table with a center leg. There are also many other small tunnels and alcoves in the vicinity that you can slide through.

Many of the mounds of star coral are covered with green and brown algae, which doesn't look inviting, but provides food for herbivorous fish. There is a tremendous number of sea fans on the top of this reef, some of them with flamingo tongue cowries attached. These beautiful animals with their spotted mantles crawl slowly along the gorgonians as they feed. Unfortunately, the flamingo tongues have been such a temptation

The walls of Cozumel are gardens of colorful sponges. Visibility here often exceeds 150 feet (45 m).

for divers that they have become scarce in some areas. They should remain on the sea fan and not in your pocket.

A few kicks away from the mooring is a nice growth of elkhorn coral where many damselfishes and banded butterflyfish take refuge. Also in this neighborhood, still very close to the mooring line, is the residence of a 6-foot (2 m) green moray eel. He moves from hole to hole and won't be found in the same spot every day. Don't put your hands in any holes without looking first.

Near the mooring line is a very large archway—30 feet (9 m) wide and 10 feet (3 m) high—that opens onto a sand flat. A 5-foot (1.5 m) bull shark is often seen in this area as are eagle rays.

50. CORONA

DEPTH:	70-90 FEET
	(21-27 M)
DISTANCE:	15 MINUTES
LEVEL:	INTERMEDIATE TO
	ADVANCED

Another dive spot inexplicably named for a famous Mexican beer, Corona is known for its large schools of porkfish.

Photo tip. Porkfish are an ideal subject for photographers, since they will let divers approach as close as 6 feet (2 m), and all tend to keep swimming in the same direction. For best shooting results swim in the same direction as the school. Be aware that they have silver scales that are reflective and can cause burning unless you use a very low power setting on your strobe.

The resident Bermuda chubs will follow divers acting as though they are looking for food, a consequence of the fish feeding that was prevalent a few years ago. Midnight parrotfish, grazing on the coral, and large whitespotted filefish are other attractions of Corona.

A view of the crystal clear waters of Cancun's prime snorkeling area can be seen from the top of the village's newest building.

51. EL PASO

DEPTH:	15-45 FEET
	(5-14 M)
DISTANCE:	10 MINUTES

This site, located just to the right outside the channel, can be murky if the sea is rough. However, on a clear day it is an interesting dive that has the added plus of being shallow, thus extending bottom times.

El Paso is a long coral ridge that rises 10 to 15 feet (3-5 m) from a sandy bottom. Most of the ridge is made up of mountainous star, brain, flower and sheet coral. Squirrelfishes can be seen hiding out in or near the many caverns in the coral and surgeonfish patrol around their territory. On the top of the ridge are some nice clusters of elkhorn coral.

Similar in size and appearance to the queen angelfish, the blue angelfish is one of the prettiest in the Caribbean.

CHAPTER **X** PLAYA BLANCA

Mexico

PAST AND PRESENT

Playa Blanca, meaning "white beach," is located on the Pacific Coast in the Mexican state of Jalisco. It is 60 miles (97 km) north of the port town of Manzanillo and 120 miles (194 km) south of Puerto Vallarta. Manzanillo, which means "chamomile" in Spanish, was brought to the public's attention in 1974, when a Bolivian tin magnate created a retreat that drew an international social crowd.

The existing resorts around Manzanillo are spread out, with much of the land remaining largely undeveloped.

The famous resort of Las Hadas—"The Fairies"—is in Manzanillo. With its white-domed buildings, Las Hadas can seem like a mirage when viewed from the sea in the hot noonday sun.

Puerto Vallarta, on the edge of the Sierra Madre range, is one of the most popular vacation spots in Mexico. In the 1950's it was a hideaway for the very wealthy, but since the filming of "The Night of the Iguana," it has been transformed from a quiet fishing village into a well-known tourist attraction. The downtown beach area, know as Old Town, remains quaint with its cobblestone streets and small shops, restaurants and white painted houses.

The state of Jalisco is known for its leather goods and silver work, and the *mariachis* and dancers which come from Guadalajara.

USEFUL INFORMATION

Climate. Playa Blanca has a tropical climate. In the winter months of December through March daytime highs can be expected to be in the mid-80'sF (29-30°C), while overnight lows will be in the low to mid-70'sF (22-25°C). For the remaining months, daytime temperatures will range from the high 80'sF to low 90'sF (31-34°C). At night the temperature will hover in the mid to high 70'sF (23-26°C). May through August are the hottest months.

Currency. The Mexican peso is the official currency, although most hotels, restaurants and shops accept travelers checks and major credit cards.

Electricity. Standard voltage is 110 volts with American-style sockets.

Entry and Exit Requirements. Valid passports or an original birth certificate and photo ID are required as is a return ticket. Children traveling with one parent must have a notarized statement from the other parent authorizing travel outside the United States.

Etiquette. Casual, light attire is the norm, and nude or topless bathing is forbidden in Mexico.

Getting There. You can fly either to the airport of Manzanillo which is 60 miles (97 km) from the village and a 90-minute taxi ride which costs about US$65, or you can fly into Puerto Vallarta which is 120 miles (194 km) from the village and a three-hour taxi ride costing about US$150. Check with your travel agent for airlines going to these cities. When you make your Club Med reservations you can buy a package which provides air travel and transfer to the village.

Language. Spanish is the national language. English, French and Spanish are spoken in the village.

Sightseeing. There is a plane trip to Guadalajara (the City of Roses) which is the capital of the state of Jalisco. It is famous for its beautiful handicrafts, and is the birthplace of the *mariachis.* Also of interest here is the colonial architecture and glass blowing.

Located on Chamela Bay, Playa Blanca offers a variety of water sports in a relaxed environment .

Another trip is to Manzanillo for shopping, which includes a visit to the scenic overlook at El Mirador. To experience open air markets of a typical fishing village, visit the nearby Barra de Navidad.

For nature lovers there is a 90-minute cruise to Bird Island, an unspoiled sanctuary.

DINING OUTSIDE CLUB MED

La Viuda   No Phone

La Viuda, which in Spanish means "widow," is about 12 miles (19 km) from the Club on the road to Puerto Vallarta in the city of Chamella. A wide variety of authentic Mexican dishes is the specialty of this casual and inexpensive restaurant. La Viuda is known for its mescal, a cactus-based alcohol which is like tequila but even stronger.

La Sirena   No Phone

La Sirena, meaning "the mermaid," is on the beach past the city of Chamella. It offers Mexican specialties and seafood dishes such as *ceviche de caracol* (raw conch in lemon juice). This is a thatched roof restaurant cooled by the breeze blowing off the ocean. To get there go north from Club Med, pass Chamella and make a left to Pueblo Punta Perrula. Prices are inexpensive.

Playa Rosa   No Phone

Playa Rosa is an expensive restaurant next to the Hotel Careyes, only a five-minute drive from Club Med. The atmosphere is Mexican, but is more adapted to tourists than the previous two restaurants. Located on the beach, Playa Rosa serves excellent chicken and seafood dishes cooked Mexican style.

THE CLUB MED VILLAGE

Playa Blanca, built on 50 acres (20 ha), opened in 1974 with room for 590 guests. It was renovated in 1987. The cobblestone road leading to the village entrance offers views of lush tropical vegetation. The fountain marking the welcome plaza in the center of the village is surrounded by large voyager trees.

At the center overlooking the large swimming pool is the bar, which also has a view of the outdoor amphitheater used for

Kayaking and sailing are two popular water sports offered at Playa Blanca.

dancing and evening events. The main theater is next to the dance floor, and offers different shows nightly with a renowned Mexican folkloric dance troupe accompanied by a *mariachi* band appearing once a week.

The main restaurant over the bar and theater is decorated with a Mexican motif, and offers buffet-style breakfast, lunch and dinner, with international food and Mexican specialties. Some of the tables of eight overlook the ocean and swimming pool.

There are two annex restaurants. The Pelicano, which is next to the sailing shack, serves late breakfast and late lunch, and is open for dinner (dinner revolves around a different theme each night). The Pelicano has an ocean view with tables for two or more. Dinner is served at the table. The Zapata is on the hillside overlooking the bay and is only open for dinner. It specializes in grilled fish or meat "Tex-Mex" style. Although there is no additional charge, dinner reservations are necessary for both annex restaurants.

Brightly colored bougainvillea grows on the

LOGGERHEAD SEA TURTLES

Summer is the peak season for the egg laying ritual of the loggerhead sea turtle on the beaches near Playa Blanca. The females come ashore and using their flippers dig a hole about two feet (62 cm) deep above the high water mark. Inside the hole they will deposit anywhere from 50 to 150 eggs about the size and shape of Ping Pong balls. After covering the eggs they return to the sea.

The incubation period varies between 30 to 60 days depending on the temperature. The turtle babies usually hatch on the same day and remain hidden in their holes until nightfall when they begin a desperate scramble to the sea. At night they are safer from birds like seagulls, but crabs and other predators take their toll.

Even of those that do reach the water, few will survive, but those that reach maturity can weigh up to 300 pounds (136 kg). The loggerhead is an endangered species. Even though its flesh has no commercial value, it is still eaten locally, and the turtle's shell is made into combs, earrings and other jewelry. It is illegal to bring any of these items into the United States.

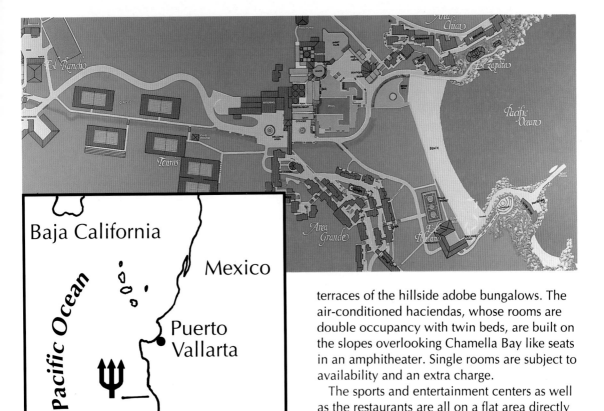

terraces of the hillside adobe bungalows. The air-conditioned haciendas, whose rooms are double occupancy with twin beds, are built on the slopes overlooking Chamella Bay like seats in an amphitheater. Single rooms are subject to availability and an extra charge.

The sports and entertainment centers as well as the restaurants are all on a flat area directly behind the beach. There are six composition tennis courts, four of which are lit for night

Equipment has recently been upgraded at most Club Med locations. Tanks usually remain on board the dive boat.

Giant damselfish are commonly found swimming under and around the dock by the scuba shack.

Scuba lessons are conveniently held off the dock near the scuba shop.

play. Volleyball, basketball, aerobics, gymnastics, stretching, bodybuilding, archery, bocci ball, sailing, kayaking and field hockey are all available. There is also a circus school and a rock climbing training wall at Playa Blanca. For an extra charge, there are intensive horseback riding programs, massage, arts and crafts, golf, deep-sea fishing, and sunset cruises.

This village is not recommended for children, however, they are accepted from age 12.

Laundry facilities, irons and ironing boards, and ice machines are available.

DIVING—TRAINING ONLY

Boats. There is no dive boat; all dives are conducted directly off the pier.

Certification. PADI and NAUI open water certification is conducted free of charge. All classes are taught right off the pier at the scuba diving shack, or in the pool if the seas are rough. For those wanting a less intensive program, the Club Med resort certification is also available free.

At the completion of the PADI or NAUI course, a barbecue is given at the scuba shack for the divers and their guests.

Equipment. Scubapro buoyancy compensators, regulators, gauges and octopus rigs are standard. Tanks are aluminum 80's, and masks and fins are Beuchat. Wet suits are provided free.

Dive Schedule. There are no open water dives other than training dives available at this village.

Facilities. Classroom work is done in an air-conditioned conference room near the village center.

At the scuba shack, freshwater showers and gear storage is available. Weight belts and tanks are kept on a rack outside the shack which is about 50 feet (15 m) from the pier entry.

There are two compressors; one at the shack and a smaller one at the pool.

Safety. Oxygen and first aid equipment is maintained at the dive site, and instructors and divemasters are trained in emergency medical care. A doctor is on call.

Snorkeling. A 40-foot (12 m) V-hull cabin cruiser, which can carry up to 30 snorkelers, makes two trips a day to local sites within a 20-minute range of the village.

Despite the fact that the water is not very clear—averaging 30 to 50 feet (9-15 m) in visibility—the marine life is abundant. It is common to see large manta rays and schools of jacks swimming by offshore.

Close to the coast the large boulders and rock formations create walls, tunnels and caverns that offer sanctuary to a colorful population of fishes, including giant hawkfish, Mexican hogfish and king angelfish.

Snorkelers with a sharp eye can distinguish the green moray eels poking their heads out of their rocky crevices. Their color blends well with the greenish-brown algae covering the rocks. The area is also known for its sea turtle population. They can sometimes be seen mating on the surface or swimming just a few feet below.

Visibility. The visibility ranges from 30 to 50 feet (9-15 m).

Water Temperature. During the winter months the water temperature ranges from the low to mid-70'sF (22-25°C), rising in the summer to a high of 80°F (27°C).

DIVE SITES

Although there are only training dives conducted at this village, you will still get a chance to observe the marine life at the training site.

52. THE DOCK

DEPTH:	10-20 FEET
	(3-6 M)

The depth of the sandy area at the end of the dock where training is held is about 10 feet (3 m). On line with the dock at about 60 feet (18 m) out where the water is deeper you will come to a large slab of rock about 150 feet (45 m) long and 12 feet (4 m) high. In this small area is an impressive concentration of marine life.

The very common giant damselfish is likely to be the first fish that you will spot since its blue robe contrasts with the brownish environment. Another is the porcupinefish, which are accustomed to divers and can be observed for long periods without becoming alarmed. The Pacific boxfish, a cousin of the trunkfishes in the Caribbean, is another of the marvels that you'll definitely see, along with the flag cabrilla, a small grouper with a green body spotted with white.

Getting closer to the rock will reveal the small coral hawkfish. This magnificent red-spotted fish is usually found hiding in small recesses. Its big brother, the giant hogfish, can normally be found immobile at the entrance of his cave trusting his camouflage ability. You can swim by and he won't move, but if you approach him he will disappear in a split second.

Another variety of fish commonly seen here is the yellow surgeonfish, named for his yellow tail. Look for the antennae of spiny lobsters protruding from their lairs. One of the lobster's most efficient predators, the octopus, is another frequent visitor to this rock slab.

Look, but don't touch, is an apt rule here as well as at other dive sites, for there are green morays in the vicinity of the dock. Although not an aggressive animal, it might become defensive if you suddenly stuck your hand in its hole.

CHAPTER XI ELEUTHERA

Bahamas

THE PAST

The Bahamas consists of over 700 islands, all of which have beautiful beaches, calm waters and sunshine year-round. Many of the smaller islands remain uninhabited and each has its own distinct personality. Eleuthera, located 60 miles (97 km) east of Nassau, is one of the most beautiful islands in the Bahamas. It is 90 miles (145 km) long and averages one to three miles (1.6-5 km) wide, except at the extreme northern and southern areas.

The English, convinced that the Bahamas had strategic importance, began settling there in the 1620's. In 1647 William Sayle, the Governor of Bermuda, published a leaflet advertising the advantages of living in Eleuthera. Soon after, a party of 70 settlers and 28 slaves, led by the Governor himself, set sail for the island. The group, who called themselves the Eleutherian Adventurers, were shipwrecked on the island's reefs, but managed to get ashore to found the first permanent settlement in the Bahamas.

The Bahamas soon became the home port to at least 1,000 pirates, including Capt. Edward Teach (the infamous Blackbeard). To rid the islands of these outlaws, the British appointed Woodes Rogers as the First Royal Governor of the Bahamas. He succeeded in driving them from Bahamian waters.

THE PRESENT

The present native Bahamians trace their ancestry to early English colonists, British loyalists who fled the United States after the American Revolution, and southerners who came during and after the United States Civil War, bringing their slaves. Other Bahamians are descended from Africans who were put ashore by English sea captains when slavery was abolished by Britain in 1834.

Eleuthera, as part of the Bahamas, was a British Crown Colony until its independence on July 10, 1973, when the Bahamas adopted a new constitution and became a sovereign nation within the Commonwealth of Nations.

Today the island's main industry is tourism. Besides the pink sand beaches, it is also known to have the best waves for surfing in the Bahamas. It has one main road called Queen's Highway, which runs down the middle of the island making touring easy. Although motor vehicles are driven on the left side of the road the steering wheel is on the left side as in the United States.

USEFUL INFORMATION

Climate. Highs during the winter months reach about 79°F (26°C) dropping to a low of about 64°F (18°C) overnight. Daytime highs hover close to 90°F (32°C) in the summer, while overnight lows are in the mid-70'sF (23-25°C).

Currency. The Bahamian dollar, which is equal in value to the U.S. dollar, is the official currency, but U.S. dollars are also accepted, as are major credit cards. Collectors and non-collectors alike will find Bahamian currency interesting with its $3 bill, square 15 cent pieces and fluted 10 cent pieces.

Electricity. Standard voltage is 110 volts with U.S. type outlets.

Entry and Exit Requirements. Citizens of the United States, Canada, the United Kingdom and Commonwealth States do not need passports, as long as the visit does not exceed

Afternoon scuba lessons are held daily in the clear shallow water of the marina.

three weeks. Adequate identification such as a birth certificate is required as is a return ticket. Driver's licenses are not accepted as identification. There is a $13.00 departure tax, but children under the age of 3 years are exempt.

Etiquette. The people of the islands are friendly and helpful. If the service seems unhurried at times, the relaxed and casual pace can help you unwind. The dress code is informal. Topless sunbathing is not permitted.

Getting There. Many major airlines provide regularly scheduled service to Eleuthera. During the winter there are Club Med charters from New York.

The nearest airport to the Club Med village is Governor's Harbour, approximately eight miles (13 km) away—a 15-minute, $25 taxi ride. A second airport is at Rock Sound, which is 31 (50 km) miles away from the village. The drive takes about 45 minutes and costs $45 by taxi.

Language. English is the national language with English and French spoken at the Club.

Sightseeing. A tour of the island will stop at Gregory Town. Here only a strip of road wide enough for a car to pass separates the turquoise waters of the lee side of the island with the blue open ocean side.

Two small islands off Eleuthera's northern coast are Harbour Island and Spanish Wells. Both are only a short ferry ride. At Harbour Island deep-sea fishing is available. A quaint fishing village here is one of the oldest in the Bahamas. It is pronounced "Briland" by its residents. Spanish Wells is named for the Spanish galleons that once stopped here to take on fresh water. There is a small farming and fishing town whose inhabitants are known for their seamanship.

On Eleuthera, you can golf at the Cotton Bay Club in Rock Sound, or admire and feed the fish at Ocean Hole which is located inland and is over 600 feet (182 m) deep. Fishes enter the hole through a tunnel from the ocean and return at will. Preacher's Cave, where the shipwrecked Eleutherian Adventurers once took refuge, can also be seen.

For a taste of something different, there is a plane trip to Nassau and the Aquatic Observatory Coral World with lunch at Club Med Paradise Island. From here you can visit the Resorts International Casino on Paradise Island or shop in Nassau.

DINING OUTSIDE CLUB MED

Matt & Jenny's   332-2504

For a pizza served in a local atmosphere, try this restaurant at Palmetto Point on the road south to Rock Sound, about five miles (8 km) from Governor's Harbour. Next to the restaurant is a pool room and bar. A taxi will cost between $10 and $15.

Ronnie's   332-2307

Ronnie's, a well-known bar in Governor's Harbour, serves Bahamian specialties such as chicken, fritters and rice. The atmosphere of Ronnie's is reggae, especially in the evening. Although you can walk from Club Med to Ronnie's, it is more convenient to be dropped off by the shuttle which passes Governor's Harbour on the way to the marina. From there it is a five-minute walk to the other side of the bay. Prices are moderate.

Kohinor   332-2668

This is a refined restaurant with simple decor but very good food. Try the Bahamian specialties of grouper, lobster, chicken and conch. Kohinor is about eight miles (13 km) north of the village on the road to Governor's Harbour Airport. Prices are moderate and reservations are suggested.

THE CLUB MED VILLAGE

The village is located about a 15-minute drive south of Governor's Harbour Airport. It first opened in 1979 and was renovated in 1989. The recent renovation included building a large "mini club" for children, making the village more family-oriented. The village, which can.accommodate up to 600 guests is built on 38 acres (15 ha), and is bordered on the northeast by the Atlantic's pink sand beaches and on the southwest by the marina.

Like most Club Med resorts, the center of the village is designed so everything is within walking distance ,including the large swimming pool, bar, indoor discotheque, boutique, offices and main restaurant.

Breakfast, lunch and dinner are served buffet-style and offer a variety of choices

BMED EUTHERA Your Village...

Dining in their own special area of the restaurant, children have fun talking with new-found friends about the day's activities.

including international and local specialties. A special section is reserved for children who may eat earlier with a separate buffet adapted for them. An annex restaurant, La Terrasse, is in a small wooden colonial-style house with a view of the beach. It is open for late breakfast and dinner and specializes in a fare of grilled meat or fish. There are seatings for two or more. Reservations are necessary for dinner. Depending on the season, La Terrasse may be open for lunch. The second annex restaurant,

the Marina, is located at the marina, a one mile shuttle bus ride away. An open air facility built on a wooden structure overlooking the Caribbean, it serves a buffet lunch specializing in grilled seafood and meats. It is surrounded by beautiful sweet locust trees, coral trees and bougainvillea.

The village's two-story beach and garden-front buildings have air-conditioned double occupancy rooms furnished in soft Bahamian pastels. Each has two full beds or a king-sized

Blue Bahamian skies and green velvet lawns grace Club Med Eleuthera.

bed which you can request upon arrival. Connecting rooms can also be requested. Single rooms are available at an extra charge. They should be requested when reserving and are subject to availability. Keys and safes are standard features for each room. Ice machines and laundry facilities are provided.

Not far from the swimming pool, amid the village's luxurious lawns is the open-air circus school. It includes a double trapeze with safety net and a professional instructor to ensure the experience will be a safe one for both children and adults. There is a circus workshop with juggling, vaulting, clowning, trapeze and trampoline.

Further along the walkway going towards the rooms are the children's facilities where there is the Petit Club (2-3 years), Mini Club (4-7 years) and Kids Club (8-11 years). These special clubs welcome children from 9 A.M. to 9 P.M. Activities are geared according to age and ability, and may include swimming, water skiing, tennis and sailing.

Water sports such as water skiing, sailing, snorkeling and scuba diving are at the marina. If you'd like some extra exercise, you can walk this one-mile (1.6 km) path which winds around the bay or you can hop on the shuttle bus. Eight composition tennis courts are situated near the resort's entrance. Two are lit for night play. Practice putting and hitting is available on the premises for golfers. For an extra charge, you can play golf at the Cotton Bay Club, a 45-minute taxi ride from Club Med.

DIVING—TRAINING ONLY

Boats. There are no dive boats at this village, but there is a 45-foot (14 m) catamaran used for snorkeling trips.

Certification. PADI and NAUI open water certification is conducted for free as is the Club Med resort certification.

Children's experience. Children, beginning at age 4, can experience breathing underwater on scuba in a swimming pool. With a small pony tank on their backs and accompanied one at a time by a scuba instructor, they can breath underwater while swimming only a few feet (1 m) deep. Children 8 to 14 can have the same experience in the enclosed natural ocean pool at the marina. It must be stressed that this is not scuba training, but is only a breathing experience in a few feet of water. The minimum age for certification courses is 12.

Equipment. Scubapro regulators with gauges and octopus rigs, and Scubapro buoyancy compensators are standard equipment. Fins and masks are Beuchat. Henderson full wet suits and shorties are available at no charge. Tanks are aluminum 80's.

Dive Schedule. There is no open water diving at the village, although it is possible for certified divers to go outside the village to another diving facility.

Children have their own "mini club" at the village of Eleuthera where they can experience the feel of breathing with scuba under an instructor's care just near the surface of the pool.

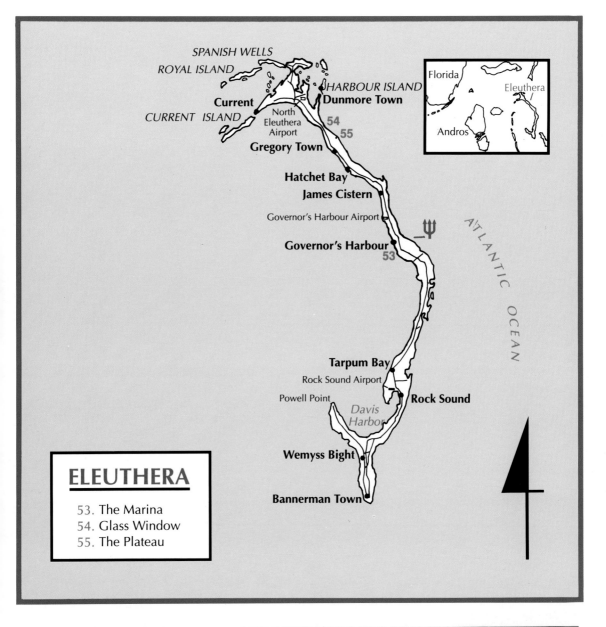

SPANISH WELLS
ROYAL ISLAND

Florida

Eleuthera

Andros

HARBOUR ISLAND
Dunmore Town

Current

CURRENT ISLAND

North
Eleuthera
Airport

54
55

Gregory Town

Hatchet Bay

James Cistern

Governor's Harbour Airport

Governor's Harbour

53

ATLANTIC OCEAN

Tarpum Bay

Rock Sound Airport

Powell Point

Davis Harbor

Rock Sound

Wemyss Bight

Bannerman Town

ELEUTHERA

53. The Marina
54. Glass Window
55. The Plateau

A perfect place for snorkeling, the marina's dock is alive with underwater life.

The exotic-looking rough file clam is usually found in narrow cracks and crevices often just off the dock.

At the end of the week there is an excursion for an extra charge to Harbour Island in northern Eleuthera. Sites such as Arch, Train Wreck and Glass Window are visited.

Facilities. There are two Compair-Luchard compressors at the scuba shack, which is located at the marina. The dive lessons are at the marina, or at the pool.

Safety. There are recompression chambers in Freeport, Grand Bahamas and Key Biscayne, Florida. Oxygen and first aid kits are maintained at the dive center. A doctor is always on call, and there is a pediatrician residing in the village.

Snorkeling. Twice a day, there is a snorkeling trip with all equipment provided by the village. The snorkeling boat takes you to Barracuda Island, Evil Island and the Caves.

Depths are usually only about 15 feet (5 m) on the Caribbean side of the village, but there are many juvenile fishes and invertebrates to see in the clear water. Close attention will reveal some outstanding anemones with spotted cleaner shrimp. Look carefully at the small sea fans where you may see numerous flamingo tongue cowries with their spotted mantles. As they move slowly along, they graze on the gorgonian stalks. Parrotfishes and needlefishes are common along the shore, and barracuda sometimes appear when they hear the sound of the boat.

Conditions permitting, the Atlantic side of the village has good, but very different, snorkeling. Right off the beach, large rock formations, with a lush array of sea fans, sea rods and sea whips, tangle together creating small passages, crevices and caves. Midnight parrotfish and rainbow parrotfish are common on the Atlantic side. Blue chromis and young sergeant majors can usually be seen darting about the finger coral in the shallow water on top of the rocks. Large clusters of elkhorn coral grow in the shallow water just a few feet (1 m) from the surface as they branch out to collect the maximum amount of light.

Visibility. Visibility ranges between 60 and 100 feet (18-30 m), depending on conditions.

Water Temperature. In the winter the temperature of the water can drop to 65 °F (18°C), rising to about 80°F (27°C) in the summer.

DIVE SITES

53. THE MARINA

DEPTH:	3-15 FEET
	(1-5 M)
DISTANCE:	AT THE SCUBA
	DOCK

For those taking scuba lessons at the marina, there will always be some time to look at the surroundings. There is much more here than you might expect.

The water is only 15 feet (5 m) deep, but is extremely rich in marine life. Small encrusting and vase sponges are growing throughout the area. On the sand, you can see many loggerhead and blackball sponges. The latter two may not be very pretty but their filtration action is equally important to the ecosystem. Close attention to the sandy area will reveal many tracks, some of which lead to the magnificently patterned netted olive snail. Look for their "periscopes" protruding as they move about less than an inch under the sand. While the temptation may be great to sneak one of these shells into your vest pocket, you should leave them in place.

This area is also rich in featherduster and multicolored Christmas tree worms that grow on sections of sheet coral and pieces of brain coral. As you get close, they will feel your presence and retract themselves so quickly that your eyes may not catch it. Wait patiently—it takes a few minutes for them to come out again. Another fascinating creature which will close upon your arrival is the rough file clam. These mollusks, two to three inches (5-8 cm) large, have red or white tentacles that protrude from the shell. You can approach them to within several inches (5 cm) before they "clam up."

Some juvenile French angelfish, as well as other juvenile angelfishes, keep residence just below the dock. No matter where you are underwater, there is always something special to see if you take the time to look carefully.

Heading north toward Harbour Island, Eleuthera becomes a sliver of land no wider than the road. On the right is the deep blue of the Atlantic Ocean, while on the left is the shallow turquoise water of the protected side of the island.

HARBOUR ISLAND TRIP

The trip to Harbour Island takes place towards the end of the week and is open to newly certified and previously certified divers. There is an extra charge for this two-tank trip which includes lunch. The first leg of the trip to Harbour Island is a 45-minute taxi ride to the north end of Eleuthera. A taxi boat then completes the trip with a five-minute ride to Valentine's Diving Club on Harbor Island. Below are two representative dives.

Distance is from Harbor Island.

54. GLASS WINDOW

DEPTH:	50 FEET
	(15 M)
DISTANCE:	10-15 MINUTES

The dive at Glass Window is at the base of the cliff where the island of Eleuthera is at its narrowest point. Only the width of the road separates the dark blue waters of the open ocean from the turkoise waters of the protected side of the island.

The dive site is on the Atlantic side and the boat moors in 50 feet (18 m) of water. At the bottom of the mooring is an area of large boulders jumbled together creating caverns and crevices. The rocks on the Atlantic side are covered with brown algae. The most common fishes at this site are parrotfishes, yellowtails and squirrelfishes.

Caution. Unless conditions are good, do not get too close to the cliff as the surge could throw you against the rocks.

55. THE PLATEAU

DEPTH:	50-60 FEET
	(15-18 M)
DISTANCE:	15-20 MINUTES

Located further south from Glass Window and 200 feet (61 m) offshore is the Plateau, a huge mountain of coral surrounded by a sandy bottom. A flat section on top gives this site its name.

Staghorn and elkhorn corals grow on the plateau top, while the sides are abundant with mountainous star, cavernous star, sheet, and flower coral. Portions of the reef are festooned with sea whips and sea rods.

A special treat on Eleuthera is diving in the Atlantic at Harbour Island where large sea fans decorate the underwater landscape.

Usually found less than an inch beneath the sand, rare netted olive snails move like submarines along the shallow flats with their "periscopes" above the sand.

Large schools of yellowtails and many Nassau groupers will come to meet you underwater. Previously fed by divers, they will often pester you for a handout. Even the usually shy gray angelfish will come straight up to your face and watch your every move. Big spiny lobsters are often spotted deep in the recesses of the reef. Trumpetfishes can be seen in the 60-foot (18 m) range hiding themselves vertically among the sea rods or rope sponges.

A large jewfish of over 150 pounds (68 kg) occasionally appears at this site, but he moves his territory from time to time. If you do see him, don't expect him to be as friendly as the Nassau groupers. As big as he is, he remains very shy. Spotted eagle rays and schools of jacks are often present here.

CHAPTER XII   CLUB MED 1

Caribbean

THE SHIP

The 617-foot-long (187 m) luxury sailing cruise ship *Club Med 1* went on her maiden voyage in 1990 and now divides her time between the Caribbean and the Mediterranean. Built by the Societe Nouvelle des Ateliers et Chantiers du Havre, the ship has five masts carrying almost 27,000 square feet (2509 ca) of sail which can propel her to 14 knots. As an assist in times of poor wind, or when operating in tight quarters, the *Club Med 1* is equipped with a very quiet diesel-electric propulsion system. Computerized ballast and retractable stabilizers reduce heeling to a minimum and the shallow draft of only 16 1/2 feet (5 m) allows entry into small protected bays where many other cruise ships cannot go.

Club Med 1 sails by night arriving at a different port of call each morning.

LIFE ON BOARD

Club Med 1 has 191 spacious outside staterooms and two larger outside suites. All have plush carpets, double-insulated walls, individual temperature control, two portholes and mahogany cabinetry. Each room has either a king-size bed or two twin beds as well as closed circuit television, radio, telephone, mini bar and safe.

On the ship's eight decks, four of which are Burmese teak, are two swimming pools, four cocktail lounges, a duty free boutique, and a health center. Massage, tanning and sauna are available at the health center.

There are many activities available including water skiing, wind surfing, sailing, scuba, snorkeling, swimming, aerobics and board games. The water sports are conducted from a stern platform that unfolds to the waterline when the ship is at anchor. The casino is open whenever the ship is in international waters or when local regulations permit.

The disco opens every night after the evening's entertainment in the main theater. Once a week there is clay pigeon shooting for an extra charge.

The minimum age is 12 years as there are no special facilities for children.

PORTS OF CALL

Home port for the *Club Med 1* is Fort de France, Martinique. From October to early May she sails the Caribbean, spending the rest of the year in the Mediterranean. There are usually four routes to choose from, but the ship's itinerary changes every season. Below are some samples of previous schedules.

Northern Route 1: Les Saintes, St. Barthelemy, Virgin Gorda, Jost Van Dyke, St. Thomas, and St. Kitts.

Northern Route 2: Marie Galante, Nevis, Virgin Gorda, St. Martin, Tintamarre, and Dominica.

Southern Route 1: St. Lucia, Bequia, Barbados, Tobago Cays, Mayreau, and Carriacou.

Southern Route 2: Los Roques, Tortuga, Carriacou, Barbados, and Mayreau.

Boasting five large masts, Club Med 1 is the largest sailing ship in the world.

Captain Alain Lambert, now with the Club Med 2, shows off the bridge of the Club Med 1 and its advanced technology.

Useful Information

Climate. Because the ship covers a large area, the climate will vary between the southern and northern locations. In general the daytime temperature will range from the mid-70'sF (23-24°C) to the upper 80'sF (31-32°C). The evenings may be cool on the water.

Communications. Ship-to-shore telephone service is available around the clock and calls can be placed directly from your room using a credit card. Remember that the link is through satellite and the rates are high. For those calling the ship from the United States the number is 011-87-1110-3120/3117.

Currency. The U.S. dollar and French franc are used on board. Travelers checks and major credit cards are also accepted.

Electricity. The voltage is 220 volts with standard European outlets, but in each room and bathroom there is a 110 volt standard U.S. outlet.

Entry & Exit Requirements. A valid passport and return ticket is required.

Etiquette. Being different from Club Med's other facilities, life on board is a little more formal. One is required to wear shoes at all times in the restaurants. During the day casual wear such as Bermuda shorts and deck shoes are appropriate. In the evenings polo shirts and blazers are acceptable for men, while women may wear comfortable linens or cocktail dresses. On Gala Night tuxedos and evening dresses can be worn if desired. It is advisable to have comfortable shoes and practical clothing for shore excursions.

Getting There. American Airlines flies from most U.S. cities to Fort de France, Martinique via Puerto Rico. Air France has direct flights from Miami. The airport is approximately 20 miles (32 k) from the ship's berth.

Language. French and English are spoken on board.

Sightseeing. Half- and full-day shore excursions are available at a nominal charge in all ports of call.

Diving

Boats. There are two inflatable 20-foot (6 m) Hurricanes with inboard diesel jet drives that can accommodate 10 divers each. These boats load at the stern platform and carry the divers to the dive sites.

Certification. There is no dive training on the *Club Med 1*. All divers must be certified and have their certification cards.

For non-divers, there is an introduction to diving once a week.

Equipment. Tanks are Scubapro steel 72's. Scubapro buoyancy compensators and Scubapro R-190 regulators with gauges and octopus rigs are standard equipment. Beuchat masks and fins, and Henderson wet suits are provided at no extra charge.

Fresh water is available on the dive platform for rinsing gear which can be stored in the Hall Nautique. The same equipment will be kept by the diver for the week. Divers are welcome to bring their own equipment.

There is a locker room with showers and towels one deck above the Hall Nautique.

Dive Schedule. There is one dive a day. An instructor is always in the water with the dive group, but buddies may dive on their own if they wish.

Facilities. While at anchor, the stern platform unfolds to the waterline creating a marina for water sports.

Safety. First aid kits and oxygen are always on the dive boats. The boats are also equipped with radios, so in an emergency they can

Spacious outside staterooms are equipped with mini bars, TVs, radios and telephones.

Luxury and space abound for passengers who have their choice of pools, bars and restaurants.

contact the cruise ship where a doctor and small boat are on standby.

During the dive, decompression bars equipped with hookah regulators for emergency air are hung over the side. Evacuation by helicopter or sea plane can be arranged to recompression chambers located on the major islands along the route.

All divers are required to stay within the no-decompression limits and go no deeper than 100 feet (30 m). A five-minute safety stop at 15 feet (5 m) is mandatory regardless of the dive profile.

Water temperature. The water temperature can vary according to location but generally ranges between the mid-70'sF (23-24°C) and the low 80'sF (27-28°C).

Dive Sites

Because the ship's ports of call may change from season to season or depending on the weather, the following dive sites are only a sampling of the type of diving you can expect. Most sites are a 10- to 20-minute Hurricane ride from where the *Club Med 1* anchors.

Southern Route

56. WHALE POINTS—*Bequia*

DEPTH:	30-100 FEET
	(9-30 M)

Located on the west side of the island, this site got its name from the whaling house built on the rocks a few feet above sea level. Whale bones are still found along the beach and underwater.

There are many juvenile reef fishes in the shallow sections of Whale Point. The slope descends gradually, interrupted by some small steps, from the surface to a sandy bottom at 100 feet (30 m). On this dive, which is a drift dive, you will encounter jumbles of very large boulders creating many small caverns abundant with fish life. Lobsters can be spotted hiding in the darkened crevices and red

Cruising to the next port of call, Club Med 1 *glides into the sunset under full sail.*

A platform at the stern of the ship unfolds to create a launching site for divers, snorkelers and other water sport enthusiasts.

gorgonians cover the boulders.

At the 90-foot (27 m) depth, there are a surprising number of goatfishes churning the sand for food. Trumpetfish are usually solitary, but they can be seen by the dozens at this site.

57. BRITTS WRECK—*Mayreau*

DEPTH:	40 FEET
	(12 M)

On the shallow sandy bottom on the west side of Mayreau Island is this 65-foot (20 m) wood and steel boat that was sunk as an artificial reef.

The hull is open so there is little risk of getting trapped when swimming inside. This wreck is teeming with marine life that seek either shelter or food from its encrusted hull. Small invertebrates lurk in the many crevices and make good subjects for closeup photography.

On the sandy bottom along the hull scorpionfish and lobsters can often be found. Also look for spotted morays, yellow stingrays and trunkfishes.

58. SISTER ROCKS—*Carriacou*

DEPTH:	10-80 FEET
	(3-24 M)

On the west side of Carriacou Island, two rocks rise out of the sea. Covering these rocks, which plunge to 80 feet (24 m), are innumerable sea fans, gorgonians and encrusting sponges. The cuts and cracks in the rocks protect large quantities of squirrelfishes and Creole wrasse. Nurse sharks are often seen resting under the rocky overhangs.

The Nassau groupers at Sister Rocks are shy and generally keep their distance. There are many different varieties of butterflyfish and angelfish—including the rock beauty—found here. Pufferfish and cowfish are some of the easiest subjects to approach and are abundant. Schools of jacks and barracuda can often be seen in the deep water off the rock wall. The visibility varies from 50 to 100 feet (15-24 m).

NORTHERN ROUTE

59. LES AUGUSTINES—*Les Saintes*

DEPTH:	50 FEET
	(15 M)

Les Augustines is a tiny island belonging to the Les Saintes group located southeast of Guadeloupe in the French West Indies. The *Club Med 1* often anchors in the Bay of Terre de Haut about 15 minutes distance by the dive boat. As a shallow dive with a maximum depth of 50 feet (15 m) it is an appropriate warmup dive to start the trip with.

The topography is made up of bouldered slopes and mini walls which drop to 50 feet (15 m). Colorful sponges grow along the walls and encrusting corals cover the boulders.

In the shallow part of this dive are many juvenile reef fishes, such as the French angel, seeking sanctuary in the many crevices along the descent. When French angels reach adult age they will pair up and cruise the reef with little fear of divers. Gray angelfish are also common here but not as abundant as the French. Other predominant species here are grunts and wrasses.

Except when southwest winds are blowing, this dive site is protected and the current is minimal.

60. SUGAR LOAF—*St. Barthelemy*

DEPTH:	10-85 FEET
	(3-26 M)

Although this rocky outcropping is much smaller than the famous Sugar Loaf mountain in Rio de Janeiro, its shape bears a close resemblance. The shear cliff dropping into the clear turquoise water is an inviting site for both divers and swimmers.

The dive is conducted along the cliff wall which plunges to a flat and sandy bottom at 85 feet (26 m). Divers can stay as shallow as 10 feet (3 m) if they wish and still have an enjoyable dive. Many crevices and caverns on the wall form protected habitats for marine life. Lobsters, crabs, juvenile reef fishes and an occasional octopus can be found by observant divers. Schools of squirrelfishes and jacks are prevalent here as well. Of the larger species, some groupers and nurse sharks have been seen here and make good subjects for photographers.

Guests traveling on the Club Med 1 *are treated to a variety of the best of both water and on-shore activities.*

The rainbow-colored creole wrasse is commonly found in southern Caribbean waters where the cruise ship visits.

Designed with a very low draft, the ship can cruise into waters such as these in the Tobago Cays that are normally restricted to smaller private yachts.

61. MARINE PARK—*Dominica*

DEPTH: 60-100 FEET

(18-30 M)

If you are only going to make a few dives during the cruise, be sure not to miss this one which is conducted with special permission in the National Marine Park.

The dive is conducted along a steep—but not vertical—wall lined with many crevices and cuts. These irregularities provide protection for the prolific fish life found at this site. Large numbers of butterflyfishes, angelfishes and Creole wrasse thrive in this ideal environment. A few groupers are also part of the long list of species found here. Swimming among the schools of jacks, grunts and porkfish make this dive a memorable pleasure. There is usually no current and the visibility is very good.

Inflatables provide easy, quick access to the best dive sites when the Club Med 1 *anchors.*

Appendix 1

Club Med Addresses

American Sector Villages with Scuba Diving

Dedicated Dive Centers

Club Med Turkoise
Providenciales, Turks & Caicos
British West Indies
Phone: (809) 946-5500
Fax: (809) 946-5501

Club Med St. Lucia
P.O. Box 246
Vieux Fort, St. Lucia
British West Indies
Phone: (809) 454-6546
Fax: (809) 454-6017

Club Med Columbus Isle
San Salvador, Bahamas
Phone: (809) 331-2000
Fax: (809) 331-2222

Club Med Sonora Bay
Playa de Los Algodones
APDO 198, 85400
Guaymas
State of Sonora, Mexico
Phone: (011-52) 622-60166
Fax: (011-52) 622-60070

Club Med Moorea
P.O. Box 1010
Moorea, French Polynesia
Phone: (011-689) 56-15-00
Fax: (011-689) 56-19-51

Standard Diving Program

Club Med Buccaneer's Creek
Pointe au Marin
97227 Ste. Anne, Martinique
French West Indies
Phone: (011-596) 76-72-72
Fax: (011-596) 76-72-02

Club Med Cancun
State of Quintana Roo
Yucatan, Mexico
Phone: (011-52) 988-42409
Fax: (011-52) 988-52780

Training Only

Club Med Playa Blanca
Cihuatlan, Costa de Careyes
State of Jalisco, Mexico
Phone: (011-52) 333-20005
Fax: (011-52) 333-20114

Club Med Eleuthera
French Leave, P.O. Box 80
Governor's Harbour
Eleuthera, Bahamas
Phone: (809) 332-2270
Fax: (809) 332-2691

Diving Only

Club Med 1
Phone: (011-87) 1110-3120/3117

Club Med Sales, Inc.

Club Med vacations may be booked through your local travel agent or through one of the contacts listed below.

Sales and Information Centers

1. 3 East 54th Street
   New York, NY 10022
   Phone: (212) 750-1687
2. 222 Sutter Street
   San Fransisco, CA 94108
   Phone: (415) 982-4200
3. Toll-free: 1-800-CLUB MED

Employment Opportunities

Phone: (305) 461-4000

INDEX

A **boldface** page number denotes a picture caption.
An <u>underlined</u> page number indicates detailed treatment.